identity

WHO YOU ARE IN JESUS
AND WHY IT MATTERS

DAN BOHI

Edited by PETER LUNDELL

BECOMING LOVE MEDIA GROUP

Dedication

This book is lovingly dedicated to my beautiful wife
Debbie and our four incredible gifts from God, Kristen,
April, Chad and Josh. Each one of you have discovered your
identity in Christ. How much is that worth to me? Priceless!

Contents

Acknowledgments

I am deeply grateful for the tenacious work of
Rev. Peter Lundell, my editor and Dr. Daniel Ketchum for
your keen eye to detail. Your work has not gone unnoticed.

I am extremely thankful for the many hours of work
Rev. Jim Williams invested in producing this book. His leadership as
Executive Director of Becoming Love Ministries is a gift from God.

I'm deeply grateful for my wife Debbie who has
supported me in this journey of knowing my identity in Christ.
I love doing life with you.

Finally, to my Becoming Love Ministries team. I will
forever be grateful for the unconditional love you lavish
on me daily. I am becoming more like Christ every day
as we journey with each other.

Foreword

Raised with bold Bohi heredity, Dan endured an auto calamity that traumatized his identity and transformed his eternity. This tragedy wrecked his body, robbed varsity athletic agility, destroyed his industry, and depleted all his currency. But the Lord removed futility, restored mobility, forgave iniquity, cleansed impurity, increases humility, grows maturity, and renews fidelity to Jesus and intimacy in the Spirit daily. Late in 2008, God called Dan into ministry with one priority: becoming love in Jesus!

The Holy Spirit called and qualified Dan Bohi to proclaim truth about identity: who we are in Jesus and why it matters. Now Dan and Debbie lead Becoming Love Ministries, teamed with eight colleagues/couples, and accountable to a dynamic non-profit board. In this team of Spirit-anointed servant leaders, my wife Carol and I are blessed to lead Global Advance among many congregations, denominations, generations, and nations.

In 2010, we first heard Dan preach at a church near Kansas City. When he spoke the next year during an M11 conference plenary session, hundreds of pastors and leaders responded for prayer. Beginning in 2012, Dan participated in national prayer summits we hosted at the Global Ministry Center (GMC) and churches in Kansas City, most recently during January 2020. To the praise of God's glory, during these 12 years, Dan has preached in more than 1,200 churches.

Carol and I first conversed deeply with Dan and Debbie Bohi during dinner at our Kansas City home in 2014. Shortly, the Lord revealed to Dan in a dream that we would resign at the GMC and move to Jerusalem, then challenged Dan to help support our ministries there. We followed the call of the Spirit who continues to flourish five new Israel related ministries in Jerusalem. Four years later, the Lord led us to move to the US to care for family and led Dan to invite us to remain on the Becoming Love Ministries team for global advance.

Then, the Lord began to enable Becoming Love Ministries to invest in other mission leaders, apostles, prophets, evangelists, pastors, teachers, ministry organizations, and global movements. These ministries thrive through partners who give sacrificially, generously, and monthly. The vision for global impact through BecomingLove in Jesus is achieving reality.

Becoming Love Ministries colleague Jim Williams invited me to help edit this book for Dan. Each section will grip and compel you to fulfill your identity in Jesus. Dan's riveting, notable insights include:

"Jesus never forgets or doubts His true identity in the Father's eyes and heart. This allows Him to never base His ministry or His identity on what can be seen humanly. He never measures His success by the standards so many of us foolishly and erroneously assume and use to measure ourselves.

"One of our biggest enemies is not believing whose we are and who He enables us to be. Believe you are who the Lord says you are."

Across ten years in fellowship with the Bohi's, the Lord has enabled Carol and me—as He has allowed many of you—to encourage, fortify, and galvanize Dan and Debbie when they needed prayer and a word of hope. We have stood beside them often with words such as these:

"Dan and Debbie, when discouragers attempt to engage you in divisive conversation, refuse to be diverted or dissuaded. Instead, stay on message: the name and nature of Messiah, the purity and power of the Holy Spirit, the Church's desperate need for Book-of-Acts renewal, and hunger of people across the Church globally for biblical integrity with living examples of loving the lost, healing the sick, raising the dead, cleansing the lepers, and driving out demons (Matthew 10:8 and 11:5).

"When some attempt to dishearten and hinder you, listen compassionately. Then, pattern your quiet, confident, and bold response after Gamaliel in Acts 5:38-39: 'If my purpose or activity is of human origin, it will fail. But if it is from God, you will not be able to stop this message; you will only find yourselves fighting against God.' Dan and Debbie, you serve the Great I AM: He alone is your identity."

Please pray often with/for the Becoming Love Ministries team. We pray together many times weekly on FB and Zoom for identity, church renewal, citywide breakthrough, regional encounter, and global impact:

1. That every participant will have ears to hear and eyes to see what the Holy Spirit is saying to the Church of Jesus Christ now and always.

2. That Dan Bohi and each team member will hear correctly how to exalt Jesus, honor the Spirit, and proclaim the Word with clarity and conviction.

3. That every person who participates will know Jesus: be born again, sanctified, baptized in and filled with the Holy Spirit, discipled to reproduce disciples, healed, delivered from oppressive spirits, and set free for family and community transformation.

4. That much fruit will remain, that each congregation will flourish long after Dan and Becoming Love Ministries teams depart, and that leaders and people of many

denominations will gather in unity, worship-based prayer, and compassionate outreach regularly.

5. That each Pastor and leadership team will be so transformed that they will never turn away or shrink back from becoming love for Jesus the rest of their lives (Galatians 5:22; 1 Corinthians 13:1-8).

6. That the Kingdom of God will be established in each city/region, so that each congregation will not be led by human empires, but we will be empowered by the Spirit.

7. That the Spirit and the Word will revive each congregation, that the Lord will impart wisdom, revelation, and knowledge, and that each will walk in discernment and bold courage by faith.

We pray for you while you read Identity now. With you, in Jesus alone, we are becoming love.

Daniel D. Ketchum, Ph.D.
BecomingLoveMinistries
Global Advance
Washington
October 2020

Introduction

i·den·ti·ty -
The fact of being who or what a person or thing is.

What is the one thing that many people struggle to answer? What are the things that define who you are? What is your identity? All of us have wrestled with these core questions at some point in our lives or perhaps we are struggling with the questions now.

So many times, we base our identity on what we do or what role we play in a relationship. And many times, these identities are created by the pursuits and passions of our lives. When we do this, we begin to limit the potential of our lives. We miss the most important pursuit… a pursuit of God to give us the identity He dreamed we would find in Christ.

As a follower of Christ, I am wrapped up in the fact that I am a child of God. That God is crazy in love with me. If I want to live my life to the fullest, I must begin with the understanding that everything I am and want to become starts with a dynamic, intimate, personal relationship with Jesus Christ.

I John 3:1: "See how great a love the Father has bestowed on us, that we would be called the children of God; and such we are."

When I began my walk with Christ I was born into a new life. I really loved Jesus and was so thankful that my sins were forgiven. Who wouldn't want this gift? I had the assurance that heaven would be my eternal home and yet there was something still missing. I desired more because I didn't have peace and joy in my daily walk.

With Holy Spirit's help, I understood that I had a flaw in my thinking. I was hoping to find my identity in people and in the things, I was becoming or possessing. Finally, as Holy Spirit illuminated my spirit I realized that I could be at rest and find peace, in Christ alone.

Dan Bohi reminds us that Yeshua has paid the price for your total deliverance and shows us the way to receive and apply this incredible gift. Let's take this journey together, you'll be glad you did!

Rev. Jim Williams
Executive Director
Becoming Love Ministries Association
Oklahoma
October 2020

PART 1

Who Are You?

What did Jesus purchase for us through the cross? More than most of us realize. And most of us don't live up to it. I think the most common reason is that we don't know who we are.

The greatest crisis in the American church may well be an identity crisis.

If you've genuinely put your faith in Jesus for salvation, He's set you free from sin, and He calls you to be His child, His brother, His friend, His dwelling place. Think about that—He lives in you!

Sin isn't the biggest problem in the church, because the Bible clearly says believers are set free from sin. John the Baptist saw Jesus and said, "Behold, the Lamb of God who takes away the sin of the world." If Jesus took our sin away, where is it?

Many of us say, "Well, I'm a sinner." No. The Bible calls us saints. The real problem is that we don't know who we are. We tend to think that what *we do* defines who we *are*. But it's what *He did* that defines who we are.

The Bible says that when Jesus returns to earth, everyone will see Him at the same time. That means He could probably live anywhere He wants because He's God. He could have a beautiful gold palace floating right above your church. Everybody on the planet would say, "That's where God lives!"

But He doesn't do that. Instead He chooses to live inside us. But look at us! We are a beaten-down-bad-part-of-town-dilapidated piece of property. And Jesus looks at us and says, "I want to buy them out and renovate them and move right into them. I want to live inside them."

This was His idea. We didn't coerce Him. We didn't get a million signatures on a petition saying, "Please come down and live inside us." It was His idea from eternity past.

And yet so many of us Christians act as if God doesn't know what we're going through. We forget who we really are, and we forget *whose* we really are and who lives inside us.

If you are a born-again believer in Jesus Christ, His Spirit lives inside you, and that makes you the highest priced, most valued "real estate" in your whole town. And your property will not go down in value. In fact, it appreciates every day because Jesus and His kingdom are expanding and increasing without end every day. There is no end to His kingdom. That's who is living right inside you. That's who you really are because of Jesus.

John 13:3–4 describes how Jesus, knowing exactly who He is, takes a towel, gets down on a dirty floor, and washes his disciples' feet. That's twelve pair of dirty feet. How can He do that? Because He knows He is from the Father and that He is going back to the Father. His whole identity is wrapped up in who the Father and He are together.

He never forgets or doubts His true identity in the Father's eyes and heart. This allows Him to never base His ministry or His identity on what can be seen with the human eye. He never measures His success by the standards so many of us foolishly and erroneously assume and use to measure ourselves.

This allows Him to humble Himself and obey what the Father tells Him to do every moment of every day through His incredible life. This causes Him to be bold, fearless, and successful in the Father's eyes.

Too many of us base our life and ministry on what we think will get the best bang for our time and effort, but if we really knew who we are in Jesus, we would base everything we do on what He says to do next.

Because we forget who we are in Christ, we get discouraged or fight with each other, and we don't change the world we live in.

Not Believing Who We Are

The enemy is our not believing who we are.

The enemy is not the devil. Satan is defeated. His effort now is to get us to forget who we are in Christ. If we are conscious of our true identity in Jesus, Satan cannot stop or limit us. Satan knows that, which is why he works so hard to cause us to forget our identity in Jesus.

I'm almost to the point that I want to thank Satan because everything he's tried to do to me has only made me more like Jesus. That would mean Satan inadvertently serves God, and he doesn't seem to know it. That's how deceived he is.

And he sure deceives people. People who truly love God can lose sight of their identity very fast, even in a moment of time. If we're not intimate with God, circumstances will speak louder than truth.

But circumstances don't set us free; only truth sets us free. Ministry doesn't set us free; ministry opens our hearts to receive truth. Truth is not a doctrine, and it's not a theology. Truth is a person. It's Jesus. He sets us free. He is truth. Ministry, laying on of hands, praying, and prophesying—all of this is great and necessary, but it only opens hearts to receive truth. Jesus alone can set us free.

Matthew 14 depicts a scary storm, and the disciples freak out when they see Jesus walking towards them—on the water.

> The boat was already a long distance from the land, battered by the waves; for the wind was contrary. And in the fourth watch of the night He came to them, walking on the sea. When the disciples saw Him walking on the sea, they were terrified, and said, "It is a ghost!" And they cried out in fear. But immediately Jesus spoke to them, saying, "Take courage, it is I; do not be afraid."
>
> Peter said to Him, "Lord, if it is you, command me to come to you on the water." And He said, "Come!" And Peter got out of the boat, and walked on the water and came toward Jesus. But seeing the wind, he became frightened, and beginning to sink, he cried out, "Lord, save me!" Immediately Jesus stretched out His hand and took hold of Him, and said to Him, "You of little faith, why did you doubt?" When they got into the boat, the wind stopped. And those who were in the boat worshiped Him, saying, "You are certainly God's Son!" (Matthew 14:24–33)

If you're intimate enough to hear the voice of God, all it takes is one word for you to start walking in supernatural ways, because life comes through the voice. Peter hears Jesus say, "Come." Just one word. Peter doesn't need a sermon series from Jesus. He just needs to hear one clear word. And then he gets out of the boat and obeys.

You and I don't need a sermon series either. We just need to hear one clear word from our Lord and God.

In the New Covenant, we're supposed to *become* the message. We're supposed to be the seed that He scatters. It doesn't matter if you, as His seed, land on thorny soil, rocky soil, ready soil, or hard soil where the birds eat you. That's not up to us. What's up to us is this: Are we willing to be dead enough that He can throw us out as His seed anywhere—and we could produce new life because we're willing to die?

In John 12:24 Jesus says, "Truly, truly, I say to you, unless a grain of wheat falls into the earth and dies, it remains alone; but if it dies, it bears much fruit." This kind of self-denial and willingness to die as God's seed is far from what we see in most of American Christianity today. I don't know where we got a lot of this stuff as it is represented and practiced.

A common one is the "sinner's prayer." Where do we find that in the Bible? Where did Jesus say, "If you want to go to heaven someday, come here, and I'll lead you in a prayer"? Jesus never said, "Pray a prayer so someday you can go somewhere." He said, "If you have enough courage and you want to follow Me, deny yourself, get your cross, and come and die. The call is not just to say a prayer and get your name written somewhere. The call is to *come and die* so He can fill you with life; heaven can start flowing through you, and you can impact this world the way He designed you to do. You would only live that way if you really believe who you are in Christ.

So on the stormy sea of Matthew 14, Peter hears Jesus say, "Come!" And that's enough. He gets out on the water. He walks supernaturally because he has his eyes fixed on Jesus. And this is possible when your gaze is fixed on one thing—Jesus alone. This is what Psalms 27:4 is about: "One thing I have asked from the LORD, that I shall seek: That I may dwell in the house of the LORD all the days of my life, to behold the beauty of the LORD and to meditate in His temple."

Looking at the Waves

When you have one focus, your faith will be made perfect. And when your faith is perfect, it's because your heart is pure. And when your heart is pure, there's nothing impossible—because you believe.

So you're walking supernaturally, and all of a sudden a big wave comes in. A "wave" like this: The doctor says, "Cancer." Or your spouse says, "I don't love you anymore." Or your kid just got arrested, or your boss just fired you, or people are leaving your church. Sometimes it seems that the waves never stop coming. But that's not the issue. The issue is never what you're going through. The issue is always about what Jesus already went through and that He lives inside you and promises He will never leave you or forsake you.

When you don't know who you are in Christ, it's always about what you're going through, and that's why we think we need more faith to get our breakthrough. I've heard many people say, "I need a breakthrough. I'm going through a season!" What do they mean they are going through a season?

There's already been a breakthrough. The stone in front of Jesus' tomb is gone! The tomb is empty! Jesus the Lord God is alive and He lives inside you.

You are the house of God. Do you believe it? The living, Most High God of the Universe has chosen to live right inside you, and He will never leave you or forsake you.

The real problem is that we don't truly believe it. Or we believed it once upon a time but have forgotten who we are in Jesus.

With many Christians who have lost their identity in Jesus, the problem is not their hearts. Their hearts are for God. Peter's heart was for God. He was walking on the water. The moment he looked at the waves, he didn't lose his heart for God. He was more desperate for the presence of God when he was sinking than when he was on top of the water. The problem was he lost his identity in Jesus because the waves were speaking louder than Jesus. So he began to sink. And so do we.

Forgetting Who We Are

In Luke 8, Jesus is walking through a crowd—because He draws crowds. Everybody's shaking His hands and touching Him. A man named Jairus begs Jesus to come to his home because his twelve-year-old daughter is dying. So Jesus goes, and along the way, with everybody mobbing him, a precious little lady comes up and secretly, but in faith, touches the fringe of His cloak.

Jesus stops. "Who touched Me?" He felt power leave Him. Apart from all the people touching Him, He knows somebody touched Him in faith and drew out His healing power.

Finally the woman confesses, "I did."

Jesus says, "Whoa, your faith has made you whole."

Just then Jairus's assistant comes and tells Jairus, "Don't bother the teacher. It's too late. Your daughter's dead."

Jesus looks at Jairus and says, "Don't be afraid." Jairus dreads the loss of his daughter. This synagogue ruler has a strong interest and the beginning of an identity in Jesus. But on hearing the awful statement, "Your daughter's dead," he falls into great fear and loses whatever identity in Jesus he had. Jairus's name in Hebrew means "faithful one," or "one who believes." And yet the moment he hears "it's too late," his identity crumbles, and Jesus sees only His fearful heart.

Jesus knows you can lose your identity—and quickly. Like what happened to Jairus—just that one statement. It's that easy to lose our identity when bad news hits us. When the doctor's office calls and it is not good news, what does the doctor's call have to do with who you really are in Jesus? What does the pink slip have to do with God's destiny for you?

Jesus doesn't judge people the way we do, and that's the problem we get into as humans. That's why there are four verses in the New Testament that say we should never judge anyone according to the flesh. We should look at people in their potential the way God looks at us. God doesn't judge us according to the flesh. If He did, we'd all be dead.

I'm so tired of our living below who Jesus says we are. Let me show you how Jesus lived. Look at Mark 1 and you'll see a guy who knows who he is.

Mark 1:21–25 says,

> They went into Capernaum; and immediately on the Sabbath He entered the synagogue and began to teach. They were amazed at His teaching; for He was teaching them as one having authority, and not as the scribes. Just then there was a man in their synagogue with an unclean spirit; and he cried out, saying, "What business do we have with each other, Jesus of Nazareth? Have you come to destroy us? I know who you are—the Holy One of God!" And Jesus rebuked Him, saying, "Be quiet, and come out of Him!"

Think about that. Demons are petrified of Jesus everywhere He goes. The demons cry out, "What do you want with us, Jesus? Please don't torture us!" Demons are terrified of Jesus. Yet a lot of *us* are petrified of demons—and Jesus lives inside us! Isn't that weird? It's because we don't know who we are.

Demons realize they can't beat God. They know they've lost. They're terrified of our Lord Jesus who lives inside us.

I don't think demons are sitting around strategizing like this: "How do we go against the angels? How do we plot our next move against the Most High God?" I don't think Satan is saying, "I think we could take God out when He has His back turned. Maybe God will forget and get careless and drop His guard." Rather, I think the devil and His demons think that they can defeat all of *us* by keeping us from believing who we are in Jesus.

I think demons believe there are few people who love God just for who He is, but that most people love God for what He can do for us.

In the book of Job, Satan says, "God, Job doesn't love You. He just loves You because You love Him. He only blesses You because You bless him. Job is like all the rest of them. Pull your hedge of protection off of him, and he'll curse you just like every other human curses you." That's what Satan believes about all of us. He was wrong about Job. Is he wrong about you?

Satan's grand plan to kill Jesus backfired. For a while there, Jesus was crucified, but now He's *alive*. And now everybody can be filled with the Spirit of Jesus and become a literal house of God. And because of the outpouring of the Spirit, we can all walk in the image of God. So I think all the evil spirits got together in a meeting, and they all just freaked out at the stupid mistake it was to crucify Jesus.

Then I think that Satan laid out a new strategy for His minions to destroy and dominate every believer in Jesus. He might have said, "This is what we're going to do. We're going to whisper and lie to every believer and tell them, 'There's no way you could really be the house of God. There's no way you can be restored to the image of

God, no way you could be the righteousness of God. You're just a sinner, barely holding on, saved by grace. And yes, someday you might get to heaven, but you'll make no difference down here on earth.'" Satan might also say, "It won't take much to convince most believers. We can get them to forget what Jesus said about them. They won't know who they are. They won't know who *we know* they are."

I think Satan said to His demons: "Let's divide the Christians and get them to criticize each other and fight each other. Divide and conquer. And then let's get them to blame God for everything. Let's get them to be bitter against God that it was God's fault Aunt Ethel died of cancer, and it was God's fault their kid fell into drugs."

"Let's get them all mad and confused. Get them fighting on the way to church. We can't defeat God, but we can get everybody to believe that they're just barely holding on, and their life is all about them. Let's lie to them and convince them that it's all about them getting their breakthrough. Let's convince them that their life is all about their big problems—ones we can constantly conjure up to harass them. If we can just keep every believer from believing who they are in Jesus, they'll forget and lose their true identity. Then they'll be no threat to us. We can defeat and destroy them all!"

Wherever Jesus goes, demons tremble in fear and writhe before Him in anguish and torment. Demons are incredibly frightened by the Jesus who lives inside you.

Mark 1:23–27 shows this again:

> Just then there was a man in their synagogue with an
> unclean spirit; and he cried out, saying, "What business
> do we have with each other, Jesus of Nazareth? Have you
> come to destroy us? I know who you are—the Holy One
> of God!" And Jesus rebuked Him, saying, "Be quiet, and

come out of Him!" Throwing Him into convulsions, the unclean spirit cried out with a loud voice and came out of Him. They were all amazed, so that they debated among themselves, saying, "What is this? A new teaching with authority! He commands even the unclean spirits, and they obey Him."

Wouldn't it be weird if we thought it was a new doctrine that unclean spirits will obey us? No. That would only seem weird if you were not intimate enough with God to know who you are.

Mark 1:28–34 continues this stuff that never ends with Jesus:

Immediately the news about Him spread everywhere into all the surrounding district of Galilee.

And immediately after they came out of the synagogue, they came into the house of Simon and Andrew, with James and John. Now Simon's mother-in-law was lying sick with a fever; and immediately they spoke to Jesus about her. And He came to her and raised her up, taking her by the hand, and the fever left her, and she waited on them. When evening came, after the sun had set, they began bringing to Him all who were ill and those who were demon-possessed. And the whole city had gathered at the door. And He healed many who were ill with various diseases, and cast out many demons; and He was not permitting the demons to speak, because they knew who He was.

That evening they bring to Jesus all who are sick and all who are demonized. So he casts out "many demons." He heals many who are ill. It all started because He healed one lady with a fever. Now everybody who's sick and demonized is coming, and the whole city is gathered at the door. That would be like your entire town trying to get into your church.

He does not allow the demons to speak because they know more than the people. They know who Jesus really is. So many followers of Jesus forget who He really is, and they forget that He is living right inside them.

Jesus didn't create demons in His image. He created us in His image.

Hearing from God

Check out what happens next in Mark 1:35. "In the early morning, while it was still dark, Jesus got up, left the house, and went away to a secluded place, and was praying there."

Think about this. How long did the service go the night before? If the whole town was there, and He prayed and healed all the ones who were sick and all the ones who were demonized, how late did that service go? Midnight? One a.m.? Two a.m.?

And very early in the morning, before the sun comes up, He's already in a deserted, solitary place, praying. He's praying because His identity is in having what the Father wants our Lord to have and doing everything the Father wants Him to do.

His identity isn't in the exorcisms. It isn't in all the healing miracles. His identity is in listening to every word the Father is telling Him, because everything He has is from the Father and is going back to the Father—it's all about glorifying the Father.

The word used here for "prayer" in the original Greek of the New Testament means "to lay prostrate." Jesus is lying there in prayer before His Father. He doesn't have carpet; He's got dirt, rocks, and grass. He doesn't care. He just needs to get back to the Father because everything is in what God says next.

Jesus is probably saying, "I need more life, Abba Father, because if I'm going to give everybody life, I've got to have more from You."

The disciples and their friends search for Him until they finally find Him. "Jesus, everybody's looking for you. Where have you been? When are we doing the next service? Man, this is a real revival!"

Jesus says, "I just spent time at my Father's feet, waiting on His next instructions. Now let's go to the next town. That's why I'm here."

In my heart I would love to go to one place and see true revival break out. I could just stay there the rest of my life. After I've been to over 1,100 churches, I find myself saying, "Okay, when can I stop going to churches and just live in the church where I am? Let everybody just keep coming in. The whole city can become the kingdom of God." But the Father keeps telling me to go to the next place. So I obey.

Jesus might have wanted to stay in that one place where God was healing and blessing everybody. But Jesus heard the Father say, "I know everybody got healed, and they want to come back, and it's going to spread like wildfire, but I want you to go to the next town." Jesus based every decision on what the Father said to do next because He knew who He was, and He wasn't impressed with what God did through Him.

If we don't know who we are, we will feel religious and spiritual and holy when miracles happen through us. But it has nothing to do with you or me or our feelings. God does it through us because He simply loves people. God can use a donkey to convey a message. He can use a big fish to save a prophet's life. He can use jars of oil to pay off debt. God doesn't need you to flow through. He can flow through anything. He chooses to flow through you because He lives in you.

In John 13:15, Jesus says, "I gave you an example that you also should do as I did to you." Jesus is our example, our model, and our pattern. His life is a pattern for all of us. First Peter 2:21 similarly teaches, "You have been called for this purpose, since Christ also suffered for you, leaving you an example for you to follow in His steps."

Jesus basically says, "My life is your pattern." You want to know what your life looks like? It is Jesus. He wants to stuff you with Himself so that your eyes are His eyes, your ears are His ears, your hands are His hands, and your heart is His heart.

Some think, "Well, I have to pray harder. I have to fast more."

No, you need to believe who He says you are. If you really believe who you are, you'll want to pray more because you'll realize you don't know what to do until He tells you. If you don't have intimacy with Jesus, you're just left with religious practices.

And we wonder why people don't want what we have.

Speaking What We Hear

Colossians 1:27 speaks of "Christ in you, the hope of glory." Hope is what we expect to happen, or what could happen if we would just believe and let it happen. Glory relates to any manifestation of an attribute of God. Here's the beauty of that verse. Maybe God could actually manifest through us, and people would experience His presence, and that would be the hope of glory. And that's why He put Himself in us because He wants to change the world through us.

Near the end of Mark, we read in 16:15, "He said to them, 'Go into all the world and preach the gospel to all creation.'" The Greek word used here for "preach" is the word *keruzate*. It means "to proclaim, to exhort, to magnify." To do that, we could say you must shine what you are, or release who you are. You're a new creature. You're not the depressed person you once were—that person died. You're not the person who used to be in bondage to addictions—that person died. You've become a new creature. Let's become the message.

Our Lord wants us to preach, proclaim. This is an action verb, but the root word of "preach" is the noun *kerucks*. This word, *kerucks*, is used for a messenger of the king who sits at the king's feet, waiting to hear his next word, proclamation, or command. Messengers sit at the feet of the throne, not wanting to miss one word. They know they are assigned to deliver the king's message to the people, so they want to get it all right. And they know that they have nothing to say or deliver to the people unless they hear it first from the king. Freely they have received; freely they will give away what the king has given them to convey to the people. Unless the *kerucks* or "proclaimer" hears from the king, they have nothing to say to the people. They must receive from the king in private before they can give out the king's message in public.

In Matthew 10:7–8 Jesus tells His disciples, "And as you go, preach, saying, 'The kingdom of heaven is at hand.' Heal the sick, raise the dead, cleanse the lepers, cast out demons. Freely you received, freely give." The phrase "heal the sick" is not, "Go lay hands on people and nobody gets healed"—and we wonder, "Well, maybe God doesn't heal everybody." Then we start making up new theologies that are not found in the Bible. No. The word "heals" here is the Greek word *therapeuo*. We get our English word "therapy" from this word. Greek scholar Rick Renner says in *Sparkling Gems from the Greek* that this word *therapeuo* means "repeated actions, such as a patient who visits a physician over and over until the desired cure is obtained." It means we don't quit until we get healed.

This means let's keep on worshipping Jesus and keep on coming to Him for healing until we are healed. Let's continue to wait on the Lord until He does what He promises He will do in His Word. Let's continue to get so filled with Him that He just spills out. You have to worship and wait on Him in private before you can do public ministry.

Jesus first hears from the Father what He is supposed to say. Then, and only then, does He speak. He says repeatedly that He never says one word on His own initiative. He first hears from the Father, and then He speaks what He hears. He is our pattern. We should do the same. Listen to the Lord and then speak.

The Father wants us to operate out of the overflow of the Spirit in us. The Lord doesn't want us to operate on our depleted selves. If you will live from the position of first waiting on the Lord and listening to hear His next word, then you never run out. You don't burn out because it's not you. You're just the channel that He flows through. The problem is we don't spend enough time alone with Him, listening to Him, loving on Him, and allowing Him to love on us.

People always say to me, "You're going to burn out."

There's not a chance. How could I burn out?

Folks say, "You're giving too much."

I'm not giving anything that's not already for you. You're not drinking out of my cup here. He anoints me, and my cup is running over. I've just given you what's in the saucer—the overflow of what He pours into my cup.

I hear some pastors say, "I'm just a burned out, poor minister. Ministry would be so good if it weren't for the people."

Where'd that come from? Jesus never talked that way. Jesus knew who He was. He operated continually out of the overflow of His intimate time alone with Abba, His Father, and He flowed in power from His identity as He continually heard His Father's voice.

So when you spend intimate time alone with Jesus, you can come out and release what you are filled with. Demons are cast out, deadly poisons can't hurt you, and people are healed. The main thing is to release Him, and let the message manifest Jesus.

The Holy Spirit Hovers in Anticipation

Let's look at Genesis 1:2–3. "The earth was formless and void, and darkness was over the surface of the deep, and the Spirit of God was moving over the surface of the waters. Then God said, 'Let there be light'; and there was light."

This phrase "formless and void" can also be translated or "chaos and darkness." That's a scary scene, and it says the Spirit of God was hovering over the face of the waters.

There's no form. There's no peace. Everything's in chaos. Everything's in turmoil. It'd be as if your spouse left you, you lost your job, you have cancer, and all your kids just died in a car wreck. Everything's going bad. It's chaos. It's darkness.

If you're not on your face before Jesus, if you're not at His feet, if you're not intimate, living on everything He says, life could quickly wreck you if you thought your life was about *your* life instead of His.

But here in Genesis 1:2, it says the Spirit of God is hovering over the chaos and darkness. It could be understood that He's crouched down. He's anticipating. It's almost like a word for brooding.

It's a word that would describe what parents do when they have a baby coming. They put special curtains up. They paint the walls. When my grandson was coming, his parents were putting up boy stuff, painting walls, and outfitting a room for the little guy. They knew that he was coming, and they wanted to prepare for him. They were brooding, excited, and in a sense, crouching in anticipation.

That's what the Spirit does over us and our troubles. Why would the Spirit crouch excitedly and brood or hover over us and our trials? Because the next verse in Genesis 1 says that the living God was getting ready to speak. The Holy Spirit is excited because almighty God is about to speak, and things are about to change for the better.

Think about that. The Holy Spirit is hovering over us and brooding over us and our trials because He knows that the Father is about to speak, and things happen when the Father speaks.

If we live in the conscious awareness of this great reality, when the worst things come our way, we'll be able to truly rejoice as God's Word commands us to do. Terrible trials would cause us joy because we know that our awesome God is getting ready to speak. He is going to speak life into our toughest trials, and what is in you will be greater than what is around you. And what the enemy of our soul means for evil—our God means for good.

Identity and Rest

Luke 5 tells another story. Peter and the boys are out fishing all night long. They're professional fishermen, and on this night they can't catch any fish.

It's like so many of us. We're working hard. We're praying. No revival is coming. Nothing has changed. In fact, it looks as if everything's gotten worse. And we just keep "fishing." We just keep toiling for our Lord. We pray, "God, we need some fish. God, why aren't we catching anything?" And Jesus says, "Let's go out in the deep. Then throw out the nets."

Peter obeys the word of the Lord, and God honors his faith with a miraculous catch of fish. He hears the voice of our Lord and he obeys. It would have been easy for Peter, a professional fisherman, to disregard the words of a carpenter about fishing. But Peter dared to believe Jesus and obey Him. He didn't make his decision based on what his past experience told him. He chose to trust that Jesus knew what He was talking about.

Why do we make decisions based on our situations or limit our faith to our past experiences? Because we don't know or believe who we are or who Jesus really is. It's all about your identity.

And knowing our identity enables us to rest in God's hands.

In Mark 4 Jesus says, "Let's get in the boat and go through to the other side." So, His disciples get in the boat, and then a huge storm comes up. The disciples think that they're all about to die. They're bailing water and are terrified. Why? Because their reality is that the storm seems bigger than what Jesus had just said. Because they're not intimate enough with Jesus to realize that when He says, "We're going through to the other side," it means that we're going to make it there, and nothing can stop us.

This storm is nearly sinking the boat, and Jesus is in the back of the boat—asleep! That little word "asleep" doesn't mean He's sound asleep. It means He's at rest. He's lying at the feet of the Father, at total and complete rest.

No matter how bad the storm is, Jesus is at rest because He knows who He is, and He is keenly aware that every day of His life is orchestrated. He knows that His Abba, Father, has a plan and purpose for Him and that the Father will play it all out through Him. Jesus can rest in the biggest storms because He knows that God His Father works everything out according to His plan and purpose.

So Jesus gets up from His nap in the back of the boat and says, "Peace." He knows that what is in Him is greater than what surrounds Him because He knows who He is.

The same Spirit that was in Him is in us.

God Means What He Says

If you're a Christian, then you're the righteousness of God. That's what the Word says about believers. Paul doesn't write, "To the sinners in Ephesus." Yet, we have doctors of theology who say: "Well, we Christians sin in thought, word, and deed everyday. We sin thousands of times a day!" Where's that in the Bible? Paul doesn't write,

"To those getting ready to make a mistake or commit a sin in Thessalonica."

Why don't we take our religious lenses off and remove what we've been erroneously taught—and start reading and believing what the Bible actually says. The-way-that-seems-right-to-man kind of thinking starts all the way back in the Garden of Eden. The first two humans are walking around, and they're living on everything that proceeds from the mouth of the Father. Then Satan comes in and says, "You know, Eve, God didn't really mean that. He just knows that if you eat from that tree, you can do everything. I know you can do everything except that one thing. But that's really what you need to focus on. Because if you eat of that one tree of the knowledge of good and evil, then you'll be like God, and God doesn't really mean what you thought He said." Isn't that weird how Satan starts speaking about God?

I wonder if that happens today. We hear a well-meaning Christian say something like, "God doesn't heal everybody. Because you know, we prayed for Bob and God healed Him. Then we prayed for Jim and he died." So it's hit or miss. God's sometimes in the mood and sometimes He's not. That seems reasonable, doesn't it?"

So we start making up new doctrines because they seem right to us. It's conventional wisdom. But it is not in the Bible, and it is not the truth.

Psalm 138:2 says God magnifies His Word equal to His name. I would say God thinks the Bible is very, very important. Every word in His book, as it is, is important to our God.

Back in the garden, Eve looks at that tree because she listens to the voice of reason instead of the voice of truth. Eve begins to think something like, "You know, that makes sense. If we did this and we did that, people would come, then we could enlarge the church facility. Adam, come here and look at this. If we did that program and got that music and those kid's deals, wouldn't it make sense?"

Adam never talks to Satan. He gets persuaded in the wrong way by His wife. And they both eat from the forbidden tree. In Genesis 3:17 God comes to Him and essentially says, "If you'd listened to My voice instead of the woman's voice . . ." Adam's response is, "Well, the woman made me do it. I was fine until you gave me the woman." Yet about fourteen verses prior to that, Adam says, "She's bone of my bone and flesh of my flesh."

What's going on? The first result of sin is self-preservation and self-justification, which both rise from selfishness and self-centeredness. Adam ends up blaming God for his own sin because it was God who gave him Eve. "It's Your fault, God!"

The way that seems right to man enters the church, and Christians lose the image of God because the whole purpose of our being alive is to be the image of God in flesh. In Genesis 1:26 God essentially says, "I'm going to create you for one purpose so you can be My image, the hope of glory." But in Genesis 2:17, He says, "In the day you eat from that tree, you will surely die."

Why Did Jesus Have to Die?

Then we come to this question: Why did Jesus have to die? I was raised my whole life being told He had to die because I was a sinner. But where do you find that in the Bible unless you twist some verses? God forgave sinners for thousands of years *before* Jesus died.

Jesus says, "If you're going to come after Me, deny yourself." You weren't created for you. You were created to be the very image of God and to bring Him glory.

So why did Jesus have to die? He died to restore the image of God in us. The moment that Adam and Eve disobeyed God and ate of that tree, they lost the image of God. They didn't die physically or right away. Adam lived about 800 more years after that first sin.

In Matthew 18:11 and Luke 19:10 we read, "The Son of God came to seek and save that which was lost." What was lost? The image of God in flesh.

Jesus didn't die simply because we were all sinners. He died so He could restore us back to the image of God so we could start being little Christs—Christians—who manifest the glory of God. . . . if we just believed it.

So in John 20 Jesus is dead. If we back up a few pages before that, we see Peter tell Jesus, "I'm not going to let You die. There's no way this is going to happen to You."

In Matthew 16, right before the transfiguration, Jesus looks at Peter and says, "Get behind me, Satan!" Jesus says that because Peter is trying to talk Jesus out of going to the cross. Pete thinks he knows what's best for Jesus, regardless of what the Son of God just stating would happen to Him. Jesus recognizes the identity of Satan speaking through one of His best friends, and Jesus calls him out right in front of everybody.

I don't think Peter tells Jesus that because he has selfish thoughts. He says that because he loves Jesus and doesn't want to lose Him. He has an earthly perspective instead of a heavenly perspective because he hasn't spent enough time being intimate with Jesus and listening to Him. He gets out of alignment with the Spirit of God.

Anytime we get out of alignment with the Spirit, we get burnt out, we get hurt, we need ministry. If we'll just stay in the Spirit, we flow in the Spirit's ministry.

When you get behind, ahead of, or apart from the Spirit, life and ministry become about you. But when you stay in step with the Spirit, He flows through you, and there is no end to His vast supply.

Men, Women, and Worship

In John 20 Jesus is dead and buried in the tomb, and Jesus' boys are afraid. They're hiding for fear of the Jews because all their hopes were hinged on Jesus. They're not in a prayer meeting; they're in a "fear meeting." But Mary Magdalene wants to go and anoint Him again because she misses Him, and she doesn't care if He's disfigured and dead.

Mary's life was spent listening and loving the Lord, and she thinks, "If I could just get back to that position of intimacy with Him, everything could change." She doesn't care what the disciples do. She is determined to go see her Lord one more time.

No doubt the disciples are thinking, "The stone's too big. You girls can't move it anyway. What are you thinking? He's dead. It's over. Our hopes are smashed." That's how men think a lot of the time. That's their reality.

Women are different. Often they think and lead with their hearts. That's why so often women lead church ministries. Their hearts are loving and worshipping their Lord Jesus. And Mary is a worshipper.

It's hard for men sometimes to worship Jesus with reckless abandon and forget about what others might think. Women are used to giving themselves to their lover, in this case the lover of their souls. It's much harder for many men to see themselves as the bride of Christ. Most men, very understandably, are not used to seeing themselves as a bride.

I hate to break it to you, men, and I know it may feel weird, but you're a bride. The Bible says that the church is the bride of Christ, who is repeatedly depicted as a groom coming to get His bride for the ultimate union between God and believers.

Mary basically says, "I'm going to the tomb to see Jesus. You guys don't have to go. But I'm going." They probably say something like,

"You're stupid. There are guards there, and you might get arrested. The tomb is sealed with a huge boulder. It's impossible to get into the tomb." But Mary thinks, "I don't care if there are guards or a stone there. I am going to the tomb because He's there, and He is my life. I don't care about circumstances. I want to be close to Him and love on Him one last time."

She shows up to the tomb, and the stone is gone. She goes and tells Pete, and he and John run to the tomb. They look in there and see the cloth that covered Jesus' face neatly rolled up. But then they leave because they don't want to hang around. It might be dangerous to hang around there. So they go back to the disciples' fear meeting. But if you're desperate enough, you'll hang around, and Mary stays at the tomb.

Mary might have been thinking, "He told me He would never leave me. I may not feel Him right now. But I'll sit here by the stone and wait."

Then two angels appear and speak to her. "'Woman, why are you weeping?' She said to them, 'Because they have taken away my Lord, and I do not know where they have laid Him'" (John 20:13).

After she says this, Jesus shows up, and she doesn't recognize him. John 20:14–16 continues the story.

> She turned around and saw Jesus standing there, and did not know that it was Jesus. Jesus said to her, "Woman, why are you weeping? Whom are you seeking?" Supposing Him to be the gardener, she said to Him, "Sir, if you have carried Him away, tell me where you have laid Him, and I will take Him away." Jesus said to her, "Mary." She turned and said to Him in Hebrew, "Rabboni!" (which means, Teacher).

Everything changes that moment she hears her Lord call her name. Just one word from Jesus changes everything.

I think she went for His ankles. She lost Him once. She's determined she won't lose Him again. Jesus has to say, "Stop clinging to Me" (John 20:17). He knows He still has to do the greatest thing. He's got to go put His blood on the mercy seat in the heavenly tabernacle. He has to get up there and finish what the Father asked Him to do. It's all about mercy. So He can't have Mary clinging to Him.

Mercy and Peace

We all desperately need God's mercy. You don't want to get from God what you deserve—that would be death, judgment, and hell. You want and need His mercy. Jesus' blood on the mercy seat makes God's forgiveness, mercy, and grace available to each one of us.

People tell me, "You don't know what I'm going through. You don't know what that person did to me. It's not fair!"

You don't want God to be "fair" with you, I promise. You want and need more than "fair." You want and need God's mercy.

If you've given your life to the Lord, then you have Jesus living right inside you. You have eternal life. You're never going to die. If you've truly received Christ, you already died and were reborn. You want *fair*? Are you kidding?

Jesus says to Mary, "I'd like to talk to you about what's going on. But I need you to go tell the boys. I have to ascend and do the best part."

Some might say, "What about the cross of Jesus? Isn't that the best part?" It's finished.

It is amazing and thrilling that He paid the price that our sins are wiped away and our bodies are healed. But none of it worked until He put His blood on the mercy seat so that our minds could be cleansed of a guilty conscience, and we can live with the reality that we're the righteousness of God.

So Jesus tells Mary Magdalene to deliver a message from Him to His disciples. Jesus doesn't say, "Go tell those no-good, fickle losers of Mine that I've got a score to settle with them because they said they'd be with me to the end, but the moment I was struck, they all scattered."

We can't imagine Him saying that, can we? He wouldn't say that because He knows who He is. He is love.

If you want to know what God is like, listen to what Jesus says and look at what Jesus does. When people turn their back on you and deny you or betray you, as Judas and Peter did to Jesus, look at what Jesus does. He demonstrates what God does to people who turn their back on Him and hurt Him. With a heart of forgiveness, in John 20:17 Jesus calls these same guys "brothers." When you really know who you really are in Christ, then by the power of His Holy Spirit that lives inside you, you can forgive others too and call them "brother" or "sister," no matter how they have sinned against you. Jesus shows us the Father's heart towards people like us who have hurt Him so deeply.

Too many Christians think they can talk bitterly toward their fellow humans or other Christians in a most un-Christlike way, and then think they deserve total forgiveness from God of everything they have ever done against Christ and His family. They want to hold somebody else forever accountable for sinful things done against them, and then they think they deserve all of God's lavishing mercy—without being merciful toward others. Why would we receive unconditional love and not become love? Because we don't know or believe who we are.

Jesus gives Mary an assignment, a message to give to His disciples. He says, "Go tell my brothers.""My brethren"is a term that means family. It speaks of covenant people. The disciples just haven't gotten it yet, because if they really knew who they were, their faith and their *agape* love would flow unlimited.

So Jesus says to Mary Magdalene. "I have to go, Mary." Then He leaves.

Mary obeys Jesus and goes to tell the disciples, "Boys, you're not going to believe it. I just saw Him. He wouldn't let me keep holding on to Him. But I saw Him. He's alive! And He is still calling you guys 'My brothers.'"

That's why you and I don't need to worry about all the things going on around the world. Worrying about all those things is the way that seems right to man.

We tell each other that we have to eat organic foods and drink bottles of water because if we drink water from the tap, we might get sick, even cancer, and everybody's afraid of getting cancer. Or maybe we're afraid about the economy or the environment or the next election or what might happen in our lives.

Why is everybody afraid? Because too many of us are listening to the voices of reason—that which seems right to man—instead of listening to the voice of truth that says we're to reign and have dominion over this planet.

This is Jesus. He's light, and He can travel at least at the speed of light, which is 186,000 miles per second, and He walks through the wall to just be there with His brothers. "Here I am, boys!"

Look at the first thing He says to those chicken-hearted guys who deserted Him in the Garden of Gethsemane just four nights earlier. He says, "Peace unto you" (John 20:19).

Why would "peace" be the first thing He says? Well, when He shed His blood and He justified us, now we have peace with God. Romans 5:1 says, "Therefore, having been justified by faith, we have peace with God through our Lord Jesus Christ," Now we can have peace with God.

The first thing He said after His atonement—after He spilled His blood on the mercy seat of the heavenly tabernacle—was, "Now you have peace." The verdict from heaven is peace.

Jesus is saying to His brothers, "Don't worry about what you've done. I covered it. Don't focus on your past sins. I have forgiven you. I didn't die as a suffering savior. I died as a representative of sin that was cursed in flesh."

Sadly, we've reduced everything Jesus did for us on the cross down to an Easter story. We want to talk about what He did instead of becoming what He is so that we can live His life.

They're all going, "Oh my word! We left You and You're back? We didn't really believe You. And then He says, "Peace unto you" *again*. And then He says this, "As the Father has sent me, I also send you" (John 20:20–21).

How did God send Jesus? "For God so loved . . ." He gave Him as a gift of love. Jesus wanted so much to become love in flesh that He spent nine months in a woman's womb. God the Son came through a woman's birth canal. That's how badly He wanted to identify with us so that we could identify with Him and be restored to His image.

He went through all the things we ever could go through, and more, because He had more to give up than any of us ever could dream. And He says, "As the Father sent me, I send you." And then He breathes the Holy Spirit on them (John 20:22).

In Genesis 2:7 when God forms man out of dust, He breathes or blows His breath into the nostrils of the dustman He's just formed. The moment His breath enters the dust nostrils, the image of God is put into human flesh. In John 20:22 the moment Jesus breathes into those boys who now have His peace, who now have His blood covering them, He's telling all humans that their image is restored.

Now just believe.

Being Dead—to Be Alive

I get goose bumps just thinking about all this, and you think I'm going to let people talking about me get me down? Do you think I'm going to let what I'm going through speak louder than what He's already done?

Think about Jesus when He's on the cross. His mockers said, "Why don't You save Yourself?" Because they thought that Jesus would think about saving Himself.

But Jesus shows us that it's never about us. Whatever we're going through is not about us. It's always been about His being glorified through us no matter what happens to us.

How could you live this life of Christ except by dying? How could you live righteousness by holding on to anything except Him? You can't. How could you be the reality of God in flesh unless you die so that your old fleshly self could all be gone?

Now you can be a brand-new creature in Christ. Six times Romans 6 essentially says, "now that you've been set free from sin . . ." It all hinges on Romans 6:11, "You need to reckon yourself dead to sin." You need to die to sin and die to yourself because all sin is based on self. So let God resurrect you in His image and in His likeness.

Some might say, "What do you mean, die?"

I just mean die. Imagine that here is a casket and I'm laying in it and I'm dead. You could come up and spit on me, and I can't get offended because I'm dead. You could come up and say, "Man, you're a terrible preacher." And I'd say, "It's okay. All I can do is look up and get my eyes fixed on Jesus. My help comes from Him, so say whatever you want. It doesn't bother me or phase me because I'm dead."

If I'm really dead, some beautiful lady could come up and try to seduce me. "Sorry, I'm not interested because *I'm dead.*" Somebody could come up and say, "Man, you're so anointed. Let's set up a tent. Let's sell CDs." That wouldn't move me or motivate me because *I'm dead*.

I'm not going to get puffed up, and I'm not going to get depressed because I am not here to be loved by you—*because I'm dead*. I am on this planet to become love so I can love you.

If I'm not dead, then I'll need people to affirm me and build me up. But if I'm really dead to self, and it's Christ living through me, all I'm here to do is to give away what I've received from Him.

If I'm really dead to me, and someone said, "Your wife just had an affair." Okay, I'm not going to cry because she hurt me. I'm going to cry because I hurt for her—because I'm dead.

Or if someone said to me, "Your kid just made a bad decision and he's in trouble with the law." Okay, I don't want my kid to make a bad decision. But if that happens, I'm not going to let it define who I am because I'm dead and Christ is bigger than that. The moment you know that you've ceased being dead is when you hear the report or you see the wave coming at you, and instead of staying at rest in the midst of the storm, you get up and think, "Oh, I gotta fight." But it's not your fight. It's His fight and He has already won.

Who wants to die? Not many people. But if you're going to come after Jesus, you have to deny yourself, get your cross (which is an instrument of death, not a burden), and die. We need to die to self. We need to die to sin. We need to die to lust and pride and anger and anything that is not like Jesus.

I'm just going to stay dead. Does that make sense? Dead to me. I want to stay dead so that Jesus can live His unending life through me and I don't get in the way with my agenda. Maybe the Holy Spirit has revealed to you as you have been reading this book that there are things you have allowed to come back into your life that cause that part of you to come back to life.

Wouldn't it be nice today to say, "No, I no longer live. I'm crucified with Jesus. I'm dead to me. I'm dead to sin and self. I'm in the casket. I'm not going to stay the same way I was before I picked up this book. I'm going out of here, flowing in His presence, because I've given up everything. Now I've got everything in Christ. I know who I am in Jesus."

If you want to truly die to yourself and die to sin, then please kneel down right where you are, and give your life totally and completely to Jesus.

This is your true identity in Jesus. Enjoy it. Believe it. Live it.

PART 2

The Gate of Heaven

When we worship in church, I've noticed that when I hold a bottle of water, and the lid is on, I cannot feel the vibrations of the music in the bottle of water. When I take the lid off, I can feel the pulse in the water. Then when I hold an empty bottle with the lid on, I cannot feel the vibrations. But if I take the lid off, even in the empty bottle I can feel the vibrations.

What if, like the bottle, we open our mind so we can be renewed with the mind of Christ so that what He's already done in our heart would become a reality all through our being? When you're dead and you're on the altar as a lifestyle rather than just being a churchgoer, it matters. Then it is His privilege to wreck your message, wreck your resume, and wreck everything at your house address. Because it's all about Him and not you.

The Gate of Heaven

In Genesis 28 Jacob goes looking for a wife, and on the way he has a dream, a heavenly vision of angels ascending and descending, ascending and descending. Then he wakes up. "Oh! This is Bethel," which means "house of God." House of God is an Old Testament way of identifying the presence of God. The angels are ascending and descending in that place—through Jacob—like a gate of heaven.

With that in mind, Jesus says in John 1:51, "You will see the heavens opened and the angels of God ascending and descending on the Son of Man." That was Jesus' favorite name for Himself, "Son of Man."

And Isaiah says to the Lord in 64:1, "Oh, that you would rend the heavens and come down."

In Mark 1:9–11, when Jesus is baptized, the heavens are opened, and a dove representing the Holy Spirit descends on Jesus. God the Father speaks from heaven, "You are My beloved Son, in You I am well-pleased."

In John 1:32–33 John testifies that the Father said the Spirit would descend and remain on Jesus. So wherever the Son of Man is, the angels are continually ascending and descending because He is the gate of heaven.

What is a gate? A gate is something you pass through to get from one place to another, from one realm to the next.

Where does the Holy Spirit live now? He lives inside every believer, which means every one of us who has given our life to the Lord is a "gate of heaven."

You are the gate because the Son of Man, Jesus the Christ, lives in you. And the only thing that can stop that from being your reality is your brain getting in the way. As soon as you shut off that relational dynamic, you're dead to the supernatural. It's our mind, our identity, or who we think we are, that limits us or keeps us from truly being the gate of heaven for others.

In Isaiah 42:1–4 God speaks prophetically of His Son, Jesus Christ.

Behold, My Servant, whom I uphold;
My chosen one in whom My soul delights.
I have put My Spirit upon Him;
He will bring forth justice to the nations.
He will not cry out or raise His voice,
Nor make His voice heard in the street.
A bruised reed He will not break
And a dimly burning wick He will not extinguish;
He will faithfully bring forth justice.
He will not be disheartened or crushed
Until He has established justice in the earth;
And the coastlands will wait expectantly for His law.

Even if you come empty because you haven't been drinking of the Spirit lately, if you open your mind to the things of the Spirit, they become a reality—the way vibrations fill the opened bottle. Even if you're not on fire, you can fan the coals back into flame.

Isaiah 42:6–7 continue God the Father's prophecy about His Son, Jesus, the Messiah. "I am the LORD, I have called You in righteousness, I will also hold You by the hand and watch over You, and I will appoint You as a covenant to the people, as a light to the nations, to open blind eyes, to bring out prisoners from the dungeon and those who dwell in darkness from the prison."

Let's follow this. Jesus lives inside us. In other words, in the New Covenant, Jesus becomes the Spirit of holiness that fills us. So we become the mission and the message and the answer for what's dying in the world around us. We become the gate of heaven for others.

Jesus' Family

In Mark 3 the scribes accuse Jesus of being demonized. His own family thinks He's out of His mind. He's called "crazy," and all he was doing was living as the gate of heaven. He is assumed to be out of His mind because He is so different in His thinking, speaking, and acting. His mind, "the mind of Christ," is what He wants to give each of us. So look at Mark 3:31–35.

> Then His mother and His brothers arrived, and stand-ing outside they sent word to Him and called Him. A crowd was sitting around Him, and they said to Him, "Be-hold, Your mother and Your brothers are outside looking for You." Answering them, He said, "Who are My mother and My brothers?" Looking about at those who were sitting around Him, He said, "Behold My mother and My brothers! For whoever does the will of God, he is My brother and sister and mother."

Notice a little detail there in that passage. His mother Mary and His brothers are "outside."

In John 15:6 Jesus says, "If anyone does not abide in Me, he is thrown away as a branch and dries up; and they gather them, and cast them into the fire and they are burned." In other words, Jesus is saying that if you don't live intimately with Him, and you think you can do it on your own, He puts you "outside." Jesus is "inside," and His mom and brothers are "outside."

So it doesn't matter about your bloodline or how long your par-ents or grandparents have been in the church. If you're not intimate with Jesus, it's just religion, and you're "on the outside."

Jesus, on that day when His mother and brothers come to Him, looks around at those around Him and says, "Here are my mother and brothers."

The phrase "Looking about at those who were sitting around Him," carries a deeper connotation of "the immovable ones who aren't leaving, no matter how hard it gets." They are the folks who love Jesus, and no matter how tough it gets to follow Jesus, they are immovable.

How many people do we all know in our churches who are there for a season, maybe a year or so, and then when times get tough, they're gone. They base their faith on what God can do for them and what He has done for them instead of what He *is* in them.

Jesus is telling us that the ones who are His mother and brothers are the ones who are going to be with Him until the end. These are the ones whom Jesus considers "family."

In the letters to the churches of Revelation in chapters 2–3, Jesus says seven times in various ways that those who are saved are the ones who overcome to the end.

The ones He calls in Mark 3:13–15 to be His disciples, He calls to come and be with Him—before He gives them the power to go and do exorcisms and heal the sick and preach the kingdom. The first anointing is not so we can go do His power stuff, the first anointing He gives us is so we can come and be with Him and be one with Him.

Out of that intimacy with Him flows the presence and power of Jesus.

Keys to the Kingdom

In Matthew 16, Jesus takes His twelve guys to Caesarea Philippi and stands near the mouth of the Jordan River, where there's a lot of idol worship. A cave there is known as the "the Gates of Hades" or "the Gates of Hell" because it was thought to be an opening to the underworld.

In the midst of all these gods people worship, Jesus asks the disciples about what other people say of Him. Then He zeroes in on the disciples and asks, "But who do *you* say that I am?" Peter pipes up, "You are the Christ [the Messiah, the Anointed One], the Son of the living God" (Matthew 16:15–16).

That is the right answer.

Jesus goes, "Blessed are you, Simon Bar-jona" (Matthew 16:17). Literally, "Simon" means "one who hears or listens." "Bar-jona" means "son of the dove." So Jesus is commending Peter and saying, "You're my son who hears the dove." Or, "You're so intimate with Me that you hear the Spirit speaking."

In the next verse Jesus says to Peter, "Upon this rock I will build My church; and the gates of Hades will not overpower it." Hades is not the problem. What you believe is the problem. Hades doesn't have a thing to do with it.

And then Jesus says, "I will give you the keys of the kingdom of heaven; and whatever you bind on earth shall have been bound in heaven, and whatever you loose on earth shall have been loosed in heaven" (Matthew 16:19). It's already done. Jesus is waiting on us to use the keys He gave us.

God knows you intimately. He has known everything about you since before you were born. Every one of your quirks, every one of your blind spots, every one of your fears, every one of your secrets, every stupid sin you have ever committed or ever will commit—He knows it all. And yet, knowing all that about us, He still says, "I love you. I am giving you the keys to My kingdom. I love you so much here's total access and total authority to the heavenly realms." Too many of us don't believe it, and too many of us don't live up to who we really are in Jesus. He has given us the keys to His kingdom!

If you have a safety deposit box at your bank and a key to that box, and you go to your bank to get into that box, something has to happen. A bank officer has to come and help you get into your safe deposit box using the key that you don't have, along with your key. It takes two keys. That officer of the bank is trustworthy, bonded and insured, and they can come into the vault room with you. You know they are not going to hold you at gunpoint. You trust them. The bank officer puts their key in that little keyhole in your safe deposit box and you put in your key. You both turn your keys, and everything that's in that box is yours. You have complete freedom and access to the contents in your safe deposit box.

That's a picture or illustration of our precious Holy Spirit. He is so trustworthy. He helps us get into the treasures of heaven. We can't access the blessings and treasures of the kingdom of heaven without the Holy Spirit. Because of the Holy Spirit you have total access to all that Jesus bought for you with His blood—because he gave you the keys to the kingdom. The keys give you total access and total authority.

A lot of times, many of us say, "God, why don't You move?" And the Lord goes, "Well, I gave you the keys. Take them out of your pocket and use them." Think about it. Jesus says, "And the gates of Hades can't prevail over, or overpower, the church." The word "prevail" or the phrase "overpower it" means to encroach upon or to collapse in on.

It's like depression threatens to move in on you, and you declare with authority and the power of Jesus, "No! That cannot prevail against me because I have the keys to the kingdom. I'm the gate of heaven because Christ lives in me by the Spirit's filling."

So what the world or Satan is trying to do to me can't cave in on me because I'm the gate of heaven. I have the keys to the kingdom.

Let's say you lose your job. "No, that can't cave in on me because I have the keys. I will overcome."

Satan tries to bring sickness into your life or family. "No! I have the keys. The gates of Hades can't cave in on me. I'm the gate of heaven because God lives in me, and He gave me all of the keys of the kingdom of heaven. I will overcome."

I think 90 percent of our prayers are fear based and not promise based. I think for so many of us, if we didn't have fear and worry in our lives, we wouldn't pray much.

Can you imagine Jesus in the Garden of Gethsemane the night before He goes to the cross praying like this? "Father, I don't know if I can go through with this. This is awfully hard. I mean, these disciples are deserting me. I'm here alone. This is too tough, Father."

Can you imagine Him on the Via Dolorosa (the route Jesus carried His cross through Jerusalem)? He's all beaten up. His skin's gone from the scourging. And He's dragging His cross. Can you imagine His saying, "Father, you know I healed everyone who came to Me. This is ridiculous. This is stupid. I even healed Peter's mother-in-law. A lot of people don't even like mothers-in-law. And Barabbas? They chose Barabbas! He killed people. Father, I'm not going through with this. Beam Me up."

That's unimaginable, isn't it?

If He had a mind and a mentality that "seems right to man," He might have said that. But the "mind of Christ" would never say that.

Too many of us say, "I'm a Christian. I'm Spirit filled. I'm a holiness person." But then we talk in ways Jesus never talked.

How can it be okay for Christians to talk in ways He didn't talk? If He lives in me, how can it be okay to think and talk in ways He doesn't think or talk? Why aren't we more like Him? If he really lives in us, how can we talk, think and act in ways He never would?

The real question is, are we humble enough to die to ourselves?

Seeing from God's Perspective

In Joshua 6 we find Joshua taking over for the great prophet Moses, who has died. He is leading three-to-five million Jews into the Promised Land. The land is already occupied with giants and great walled cities. Joshua's job is to take the land by conquest.

No doubt Joshua is thinking, "What am I supposed to do with that huge walled city called Jericho? I mean, we don't have weapons. We've been walking around the wilderness, eating coriander seed stuff that tastes like honey. What am I supposed to do?"

Unless he gets God's perspective on his situation, he will never make it. Joshua doesn't know what to do because he doesn't see from God's vantage point. As long as he can't see God's perspective on Jericho, he will never make it.

Many of our prayers are from the perspective of our problems and how big and impossible they are. We must begin to see our problems and obstacles from God's perspective and the reality of who we really are in Christ right now. According to Ephesians 2:6, if you are a believer in Jesus, and He is your Lord and Master, then right now you're seated with Jesus on His throne in heavenly realms.

You are seated at the right hand of the Father. Everything that's against you is below you. That is, unless your reality is, "I'm still down here trying to fight to earn my stripes to get there." We're already there in the Spirit, so this is what God wants to do: He wants to give us His perspective. We need to see life and our problems from His perspective.

Joshua desperately needs to see the big walled city of Jericho from God's vantage point. So the Lord comes to Joshua and says, "Look, Joshua, look! Haven't I given the city to you?" All of a sudden Joshua can see God's plan and strategy for him and his people, and he knows that they will be victorious. It may not make a lot of sense to the natural man's mind, but it doesn't matter. Joshua sees it from God's perspective, and he knows the result before it happens. This gives him the courage and determination to follow God's unorthodox battle plan.

Can you imagine General Joshua detailing the battle plan he received from the Lord for Jericho to his military captains? "Okay, men, we're going to silently walk around this big walled city every day for six days in a row, and on the seventh day we will walk around the entire city seven times, and then we'll shout, and the wall is going to fall down. The whole city's going to collapse right in front of us, and we're going to save the prostitute and her family because she'll be in the genealogy of Jesus in the gospels someday." How could you come up with a plan like that, unless you saw from the promise of God's perspective, instead of the problem you think you're up against?

Jesus addresses an aspect of perspective in Luke 11:34, the eye. "The eye is the lamp of your body; when your eye is clear, your whole body also is full of light; but when it is bad, your body also is full of darkness."

Jesus essentially says, "The lamp of the body is the eye. Therefore, if your eye is good, healthy, pure, focused, and singular, it's clear. It's not a broad way where you have lots of options. It's just one way. But when your eye is bad, your body is full of darkness."

A lot of people in the church have good hearts, but their eyes are bad because their minds are torn between two opinions.

If your vision and your perspective and what you believe the truth of God's gospel says about who you are matches what He says about you, then you have a clear, single, good "eye." It means you bought into the truth. There's nothing left in you that's for sale. Satan can't tempt you with something because you gave everything away to Jesus that can be tempted.

What you are and who He is in you is your single focus. Your perspective affects everything in you, and your single perspective and focus needs to be on what He says about you. If your eye is single, focused, and all you believe is truth and not the way that seems right to man, your whole being is positively affected by what you see.

What you see, and the perspective from which you see it, started in the Garden of Eden. Satan says to Eve, "Eve, have you thought about, umm, what God really meant? Hey, you won't really die. I mean, He was just going to try to bring you along slowly. He doesn't want you to have the fullness of His presence all at once. He wants to give it to you little by little. So why don't you just take a shortcut and buy in to that knowledge?"

Satan got in there and reasoned with Eve and talked about God. Think about that, Satan talked about God. Satan reasons with us about the Lord as well. Imagine his saying something like this to you: "God doesn't heal everybody. I know that's in the Bible, but it's just like a template that's not to be taken seriously."

I don't think Adam and Eve are the only ones who had the option of eating from two different trees every day of their lives. We do too.

Every single day we Spirit-filled, baptized-by-fire, dead-to-self Christians have the option to keep our eyes focused and eat from the Tree of Truth or to take another option of plan B that says, "Maybe God doesn't want to come through for us this time." We have the option to eat from the tree of knowledge every day of our lives. And when we do that, we lose our true identity in Christ. When that happens, we lose His perspective, and we are not living in faith.

That's why we usually don't operate like Jesus. Because He never lost His identity. He stayed focused. He set His eyes and His gaze on Jerusalem, where He knew that His heavenly Father wanted Him to go. He set His eyes and His gaze on the cross. He didn't ever lose focus on His purpose for being on earth. A major part of His purpose was to manifest the image and nature of God in human flesh. Every single one of us has that same purpose—to manifest the image and nature of God in our flesh.

Psalms 138:2 states that God elevates His Word equal to His name. Everything He says is higher than anything else. And when you reduce what He says to simply being something that happened in the past, but you listen to the lie from hell that it can't happen in your life now, you have bought into the wrong concept, and you are choosing to eat of the wrong tree, and you no longer have a good eye. If the light within you is darkness, then Jesus says that your whole body is full of darkness. He doesn't say that your body is bad. But He says that your whole body is now being affected by what is bad because it doesn't have a vision of what is true.

You have a choice. You always have a choice. You can either use the keys of the kingdom that God has given you and believe the truth, or you can keep them in your pocket and leave your life up to chance and say, "I have enough to get to heaven someday."

Healing the Impossible

I was in Michigan and a man brought his wife to the church service in a wheelchair. I looked at her, and the Holy Spirit showed me His vision for her and said, "I'm going to heal her tonight." I was setting up my little product table in the back, watching people come in, and this couple had driven four hours to get to the service.

The lady in the wheelchair couldn't move at all. The Holy Spirit came up next to me and said, "Look."

I said, "What?" The Holy Spirit said, "I'm going to heal her tonight."

So I didn't have to have vision. I didn't have to have faith. I had His perspective. I wasn't going to have to pray from a problem. I was going to operate from His promise.

The service went on, and I said, "Who wants to give their life to Jesus?" Thirty-to-forty people came to the front of the church, and the lady's husband pushed her in the wheelchair up to the front. He said, "I've been bitter at God, and I want to surrender." And he did.

Toward the end of the service the Holy Spirit said, "Okay, call her up and pray for her."

I called out, "Sir, can you push your wife up here? I want to pray for her. I feel that God wants to touch her."

He said, "Okay." And he pushed her up.

I asked, "What's wrong with your wife?"

"She has ALS, Lou Gehrig's disease."

When he said that, my heart and my faith sank. There is no cure for ALS.

Jesus didn't have the issue that many of us have. He didn't have thirty-two reasons in His back pocket of why God can't do something. Because He had the mind of God that kept His head and His heart connected continually with the heart and mind of the Father. He's the gate of heaven.

We have the mind of flesh. It has to be transformed and renewed every single day because we're slow learners and because we live in the world.

So I said to the Lord, "I don't have faith for Lou Gehrig's disease. God, what were you telling me? Because people don't get healed of ALS. It's fatal. That's what science says."

For too many of us Christians, "the way that seems right to man" too often trumps some things in the gospel because that's our experience. But it wasn't Jesus' experience, and Jesus lives inside all of us. He wants to manifest out of all of us.

I think we could be doing the same things Jesus did if our eyes stayed single and we didn't buy into multiple choices when it got tough. If we would just bind to this and believe it, even if all others forsook us, then we could be in a realm where there would be no feeble or sick among us.

God told His people in the Old Testament that if they obeyed Him and believed, there would be no sick among them. He would heal them of every disease. If that were possible in the Old Covenant, why isn't it possible in God's New Blood Covenant with Jesus?

So there in that church I said to God, "God, You can't heal Lou Gehrig's."

The Word of God says in Genesis 2:17, "The day you eat from the tree of the knowledge of good and evil, you'll die." I was about to eat of the tree of knowledge that brings death.

Mark 16:18 promises us that you'll lay hands on the sick, and they'll recover.

I had a choice. Was I going to believe what made sense to my natural mind? Or was I going to believe God's promise in Mark 16:18?

The day I buy into the logic that says that certain circumstances are too hard for God is the day I am choosing to eat of the tree of knowledge that always leads to death. The day I believe the lie that "seems right to man," is the day I begin to die. The image of God will be diminished in me, and I will no longer do the things Jesus did.

The day I believe God's truth is the day I live. The day I keep my eyes focused on Him is the day I'll lay hands on the sick and they'll get better. It doesn't matter if it is Lou Gehrig's disease or a fever.

We always have a choice. Every single day of our life. We can choose to believe the lies that Satan casts, and death and defeat will follow. Or we can keep our eyes focused on the truth of Jesus, and our whole being—spirit, emotions, body, flesh, finances, family, relationships, everything—is positively affected and blessed.

The dear lady in the wheelchair who had ALS was still sitting there in front of me.

I said, "Sir, umm, so she has Lou Gehrig's?"

"Yeah."

"How long?"

"Nine years."

Oh my. "Well, can she walk?"

"No, she can't even lift her head up or move her arms."

Then God said to me, "What did I show you?"

I said, "Yeah, Lord, but that's before I knew she had Lou Gehrig's."

The Lord said, "I didn't lie, and I'm not a liar. And I showed you I would heal her. So you need to pick up the truth and believe My Word again."

Oh, if it weren't for Jesus. Hebrews 1:2 says, "In these last days [God] has spoken to us in His Son." If you want to know what God is speaking, it's through the life of Jesus. Every single person in the Bible that came to Jesus for healing was sent away healed and whole.

Every person who came to Him for healing was healed, every single one. Nobody was left out. Don't you wish that He had not healed just one? Then we could always say, "Well, that's the one." And it would give us an excuse or an out when we don't see people healed.

So I had a choice that night. Was I going to believe God's Word, or was I going to believe what the doctors say about Lou Gehrig's disease? Was I going to believe the promises of God's Word, or was I going to buy into the conventional wisdom of man that says something like this: "Maybe God's healing for her is to let her die and take her home to heaven where she will be ultimately healed."

When I see people who don't get healed, I think, "What? Jesus would heal him or her. And You're in me, God."

The Lord said to me, "Just believe. Get your eyes right."

I said, "What? I'm trying."

"Good. Die some more."

That's right.

"I already got sanctified, Lord."

The Lord said, "Good. Stay sanctified. Die some more."

So I said to the ALS lady in the wheelchair, "Ma'am, if you want me to pray for you that you would be healed of Lou Gehrig's tonight, would you raise your head and look at me with your eyes."

And her husband said, "She can't do that, sir. She can't move her head."

I'll never forget this because it blew my mind. She went, "Uhhhh." And she rolled her head back and looked right at me.

Her husband, who had just given his life to Jesus, said, "She can't do that."

I said, "I understand she can't do it. But she just did."

So here's what was happening to me at the time: She lifted her head, and I said, "Oh, I am going for it." Because I've got weak faith.

But Luke 10:8–9 says, "Whatever city you enter and they receive you . . . heal those in it who are sick." In essence, Jesus is telling His followers, "Heal them before you preach because otherwise they're tired of sermons and won't pay attention."

Jesus tells His folks, "Heal the sick and then tell them the kingdom is there." Jesus says this because He knows that everybody walks around with options in their lives. And they don't have single focus because they're still holding onto security and they're still holding onto reputation. They're still holding onto their lives.

They are still thinking in the back of their minds, "Well, if God doesn't come through . . ." They're holding on to their circumstances and their contingency plans. "We prayed for Jim and he died." Well, that's not Jesus' experience. That's our experience.

So, I said, "Ma'am, if you want me to keep praying, would you grab my hands?"

Her husband said, "She can't raise her hands. She can't move her hands."

And his wife reached her hands up, grabbed my hands, pulled herself up, and rose to her feet in one extended motion. She fell into me, her head right against my chest. Now her husband was crying. He hadn't seen his wife move in three years.

I asked, "Do you want to walk?"

"Yehhhh."

She started walking, and she got to the point where she was walking, and nobody was even touching her, and she hadn't walked in three years. She hadn't even moved her limbs in three years.

Now what would have happened if I were to have let my circumstances and my human reasoning trump the vision of God's perspective and His promises?

She would have left that service still in the wheelchair.

Every day, every single one of us has this choice, don't we?

We have the choice or option every day to believe the truth or to believe the way that seems reasonable and "right to man."

Healing Expectations

I was at a camp meeting in Ohio, where I preached on depression. So many people today struggle with depression, and they're depressed because they don't know who they are.

How can you be depressed if you realize God lives inside you, and He will never leave you or forsake you?

I'm not being insensitive. I myself used to be depressed until I figured it out. Now it's hard for me to get depressed. I'm living the truth that I'm preaching.

Some might say to me, "Well, everything's good in your life."

You have no idea. I'm not happy because my ducks are in a row. Believe me, they get out of the row. I'm happy because God's inside me, and I'm His house, and He's never leaving me.

So at the end of that sermon on depression, I gave an altar call for people to come up and be set free and healed of depression. About a hundred people came up, all depressed and wanting to be delivered of depression.

At the same time the depressed people came up, about a 150 senior citizens, saints, holiness people, got up, went out to the snack shop and started eating hot dogs and drinking Cokes.

Here we had a hundred people who were depressed, wanting and needing prayer, and all the saints with white hair got up and left. I saw them under the tent, eating snacks while a hundred other people wanted to be healed.

At first I was not happy. I was upset and frustrated. Inside I was saying, "Why am I here? I just poured my life out. I gave my soul. And those people would rather get hotdogs and Cokes than see what God will do here."

The Holy Spirit said to me, "You're not here for them. You're here for these hundred folks who have come forward to be prayed for for healing. So do what I sent you to do."

I'll never forget it. You get marked in situations like that. God marks us, and I think we have a way of marking Him too. So when things get really, really tough, instead of looking at plan B, we just keep on looking at Him and gazing even harder at Him. We mark His heart with our constant gaze of faith and trust in Him.

And when we do that, our relationship with Him goes to a deeper level of intimacy.

So I said, "Pastors, can you come help me?" And a bunch of pastors came up and started laying hands on the depressed people and praying for them.

Two ladies were there in wheelchairs. I was painfully aware of them because while I was preaching the message, halfway through I just started weeping and crying. And I said, "God, how come I can't heal those ladies like you would?" It broke me up.

Now we were going down the line, praying for the depressed people. At the end of the line one of these ladies in a wheelchair reached the front. I looked at her and asked, "Are you depressed?"

"No."

"Well, why are you here? This a depression altar call." I said that because it's easier for me pray for depressed people than to pray for people in wheelchairs. Why is it easier? It's easier because a lot of my faith is built on my circumstances and what I have seen in the past, instead of on God's Word and *His* circumstances. A lot of my belief system is a paradigm that I've allowed to be erected in my mind based on my experiences—and not answers to prayer and what *He* has experienced. He's the one who lives in me, wanting to live His life through me. But if I truly deny myself, and I no longer live, and my mind doesn't get in the way of what He's wanting to live through me—then all things are possible through Him.

So here was this lady in a wheelchair who came up for the depression altar call, and she was not depressed.

"What do you want to do?" I asked.

"I want to walk."

"Oh boy. Okay. What's wrong with you is you have a disease. How long has it been?"

"Years."

"You want to walk?"

The Holy Spirit came right up next to me and said, "See? Watch her get up."

I said, "Oh, how's this? Okay, I'm going to get you up."

"I'm afraid."

"I'm afraid too." I really was, but I picked her up and she walked. She walked three hundred yards. She hadn't walked in years.

Now what if I'd have bought into the lie that people don't get out of wheelchairs? That's just part of life. If your eyes are good, your whole being's affected by what you see. If you believe the truth, the truth sets people free.

People have said to me, "Dan, you don't understand. Joni Eareckson Tada was paralyzed in a diving accident. She's never gotten out of her wheelchair." You're right. I'll never understand that, but I'm not going to let my experience or Joni's experience trump God's Word because that's when life starts dragging you down.

When you base your faith on your experiences, instead of His experiences and truth, then you're in trouble. When you base your faith on what you're going through instead of what He already went through, then life speaks louder than truth. Then the best we can do is compare our horror stories and leave feeling worse.

If the way you think doesn't make you more peaceful, more joy filled, more confident, more bold, then you don't have your mind fixed on things above. You're trying to get resources from the earthly realm instead of the heavenly realm.

So that lady got up and walked. Everybody in the tent was clapping and shouting, and she was walking. And all the people out eating hot dogs were looking in and saying, "What's going on?"

Their hearts weren't against God. Those people all loved God. They wouldn't drive all that way and sit in a tent in hundred-degree heat for three hours of preaching if they didn't love God. Their minds just didn't believe God would still do the miraculous. If they did, watching Him touch people supernaturally would have been more important than getting a Coke.

I don't think people come to campmeetings because they hate God. I just think they don't expect anything anymore because their eyes have been skewed for so long. Their perspective isn't the truth of the Word. Their perspective is the truth of their own experiences.

Some might say, "Well, our family just gets diabetes. You know, that's in our heredity."

I thought your old self died with Jesus, and you have a new heredity. If you're a believer in Jesus, then you are a totally new creation.

My Turn for Healing

I pulled into a hotel in Chattanooga, Tennessee, and the Holy Spirit said to me, "If you'll do everything I tell you this year, I'll heal your diabetes."

"Okay." I said, "What do you want me to do?"

He said, "Walk, walk, walk."

So I went to the exercise room and walked ten minutes on the treadmill, and thought I would have a heart attack. Ten minutes and I felt like I was going to die because I hadn't exercised in twenty years.

That was January 3. On February 19 I'd been walking for a month and two weeks. I got done walking that day and I had walked three miles. I showered and lay on my bed in the hotel room, and the Holy Spirit came in the room and said, "You don't have to take your shot tonight. I've healed your diabetes."

That night I had everybody pray for me because I didn't want to die of diabetes or lose my feet. I wanted to live long. I wanted to be a grandpa. I wanted to be a husband. I wanted my ministry to go on. I. I. I. I.

My prayers were based on what I wanted, and they were motivated mostly by worry and fear because my dad was on three times the insulin I was.

My prayers were not motivated from the promise that by His stripes, I'm healed. The Word says that I died with Christ, and I live in righteousness. My prayers weren't motivated from the promise or the position I have in Christ. My prayers were motivated from my problem and my fears.

There I was in that room. Now I'd heard from the Lord that He had healed my diabetes and that I didn't need to take my shot of insulin. The first thing I did when the Holy Spirit spoke that to me was to call my dad because that's what we always do.

We checked it out in the flesh. "Dad, what do you think? I feel that God told me He's going to heal my diabetes now—if I don't take my shot."

Dad gave me great wisdom. "Well, if it's God, you're happy. If it's not you're in trouble."

I felt peace because Jesus says in this world we will have trouble but He has overcome the world (John 16:33).

Psalms 34:19 says, "Many are the afflictions of the righteous, but the LORD delivers him out of them all." He will do that if we keep our focus single and on Him.

So I did not take my insulin shot. The next morning I got up and checked my sugar. Normally it would be over 200, and it would drop below 150 with 50 units of insulin a day. But on this day, without my shot, it was 115. Had God healed me? Or was this just a fluke?

"Oh well, that's just a fluke. It's still in my system." This is the kind of thinking "that seems right to man" that leads to death.

I preached the next day. Checked it. No sugar problem. "Well, it's taken a while to get out of my system." It seemed right to me.

No. I got healed.

I have not had a shot since that day. Jesus healed me.

I didn't get healed because I prayed harder. I didn't earn it. He already bought it. I believe there are people reading this book who have been battling things in their lives for years and years. I did too.

When the Spirit spoke, it was as if He came up next to me and showed me His vantage point, His vision, His perspective. My eyes got more focused, and all I could see was what He said. And I had a choice. Would I believe what He said? Or would I just believe that I have diabetes because that's what science, my family medical history, and the doctors told me?

Fear Prayer and Thanksgiving Prayer

One time my baby girl, Kristen, was in trouble, and she wanted a divorce. It ripped my heart right out of my spirit, and I was in fear. I lived in fear. I wanted to go home. I didn't want to travel anymore.

I said, "God, you told me if I would seek Your kingdom and Your righteousness, You'd look after mine. It seems You've let me down."

He hadn't let me down. I just forgot who I really was.

He can't let you or me down because He's love, and love never fails. What lets you down is your belief and your vision and your focus on who you think He is in you.

Sometimes I think, "I'm going to start sending out emails because if I could get 20,000 people or more praying, it would give God a better chance. If we could get 20,000 to come to a big auditorium to pray, maybe God could bring revival." We think and act as if the Bible has God saying, "If you could get 20,000 or 30,000 together to pray, then I could probably save the city." You know what the Bible says? It says that if just one person would believe what Jesus said, then any mountain would be moved.

Some want to say, "We don't want to pray because it doesn't work." Why doesn't it work? "Well, we just can't get more than fifteen to come to a prayer meeting."

Jesus said that if just two or three of you get together that He is with you. With fifteen at prayer meeting, you have God's odds beat by five times (Matthew 18:20).

If you have fourteen to fifteen agreeing with you in prayer at your prayer meeting, then you have seven-plus times more than Jesus said was necessary to see heaven move on your behalf (Matthew 18:19).

So in fear and in doubt we send out our prayer requests. We try to elicit prayer warriors to pray for us, because we think we're in trouble.

I asked myself, "Why am I preaching to lots of people in church after church if I can't get my own daughter saved and right with God?"

But I have a choice. You have a choice. This choice is before us, every single day of our lives. Will we choose to have a single eye focus or a divided eye? We never lose the ability to choose. It's there every single day. Multiple times a day we have a choice.

For five months I went to fear praying for my daughter. There are people reading this book who have been praying in fear for years. God doesn't typically answer fear-based prayers. Most of those prayers don't even get through the ceiling.

If you really don't believe God can or will answer you, then you are praying in fear. You wouldn't be in fear if you knew for a fact that God was answering you.

While I was lying in my hotel one night, God spoke to me. "Why don't you start thanking Me?"

"For what?" I asked.

"Because I'm working in your daughter's life. You don't think like Me; you're looking at what you can see. You're not looking from My perspective."

If we see our problem from God's vantage point, that changes everything.

The Lord said to me, "I want you to unleash some worship and some praise and some thanksgiving."

I started saying to the Lord, "Okay, I'll thank You, God. I don't know what I'm thanking You for, but I'll just thank You for working in my daughter and thank You that You gave her to me. She's not even mine. When she was a baby I dedicated her to You. So what am I worried about? She's Your kid."

I was reminded that the Holy Spirit was in me. So I worshipped. I praised, and I gave God great thanksgiving. I asked the Lord, "What do I do with this fear and doubt and worry?"

"Get rid of it. Bind it."

"Okay."

About a week went by and I got a call from her. She said, "I don't know what I was thinking. I forgot who I was. It's not about me." She was delivered. She was changed.

Was it the five months of fear and prayer, or was it the week of belief and thanksgiving? You know which.

Speaking the Truth in Love

A friend of mine told me that his wife confessed to an affair she'd had ten years earlier, and in his anger and pain he went off into sin.

He started drinking a little bit and smoking dope. It's not even like him. Obviously he forgot who he was because if he were on fire for God and remembered who he really was in Christ, he wouldn't have gone stupid for a while. But he was so broken. He was looking at his situation as if he weren't a new creature in Christ Jesus. He knew Jesus, but he had lost his identity in Christ. For a little while he forgot who he really was.

I didn't know how to respond to him.

God said to me, "Don't judge him by the flesh. Look at Him. Just look. Look at him the way I look at him."

I said, "What do you mean?"

The Lord said to me, "He wouldn't feel bad about that if he were evil. He feels bad because there's righteousness in Him trying to conform to the image of God. When he was a sinner, he didn't feel bad about it. But now he feels so bad because he's no longer a sinner. He's a saint that forgot who he was."

This guy kept bugging me and crying. "I don't know what I'm going to do. I want a divorce."

I said, "Why? Jesus didn't divorce you when you forgot who you were and you went into sin."

He said, "I don't know if I can trust her."

"So what?"

"Well, I'm hurt."

"Why?"

He got mad at me, and I was kind of in trouble because he was a big supporter of my ministry, and I was being real with Him. I didn't want to cater to His money because there's nothing in me that's for sale.

I said, "Dude, you shouldn't be hurt. You shouldn't be crying because of what she's done to you. You should be crying because of who she is right now away from Jesus. You should be hurt for her."

The church has bought into this wisdom of the world, and we give out the wisdom of the world to each other when we're in trouble or pain. We call it "wisdom" because it makes sense. It seems right to man.

We make people out to be victims or perpetrators. But if we just let people die and really be born again in Christ and stop loving their own lives and give their lives up to death, everything would change.

As a Christian you no longer have rights. You have given up your rights to Jesus. Because Jesus loves you, you don't need your wife or your husband to validate you or complete you. You are not here to be loved by them. You are here to love them.

If we're really dead to ourselves and alive in Jesus, why are we so hurt?

Some might say to me, "You're being insensitive."

No, I'm not. Because I used to be hurt and depressed too. I used to live in fear. I used to be sick. But that old me died with Christ. I'm in the casket.

"That's scary."

Good. Fear can motivate you to change, maybe even be the gate of heaven.

I wish my kids always made good decisions. I wish the money were always abundant. I wished the car didn't break down. And I sometimes wish I got along better with my wife. But those temporary issues and problems don't change the fact that He created me to be in His image. He lives right inside me. My temporary problems don't change the fact that He wants me to be the gate of heaven for others.

So the man who was broken because of his wife's infidelity called me back. He was crying. He said, "Thanks for speaking the truth to me. I don't need to get a divorce. I need to love her and not hurt her. She forgot who she was."

Jesus didn't always coddle people in their broken state. He would speak truth to them in love.

"The way that seems right to man" causes us to want to come around and only comfort hurting people. Sometimes the best comfort is: "No. That's not who you are."

This dear brokenhearted brother said to me, "I can never get divorced. She didn't know who she was. God broke her heart, and that's why she confessed it. Ten years later, she's righteous. She's holy. I got hurt because it was about me. But it's not about me. It's all about Him."

You might ask, "Was it scary when you were telling him that stuff?"

A little bit. It was a little dicey because he's a part of my security. But really he's not. The Lord is my security.

Your Reality in the Heavenly Realm

Whatever we are facing, Jesus can deal with it. An unfaithful spouse, a daughter or son in trouble, Lou Gehrig's disease—it doesn't matter. Our Lord Jesus can handle it all if we remember who we are in Christ and who lives inside us.

We don't have to give in to worry and doubt. There's no way that needs to happen if we remember who we really are and who lives inside us. When we remember that Jesus gave us the keys to the kingdom, and lives inside us, then right now we can be the gate of heaven, both for ourselves and for others.

You will never truly use the keys to the kingdom unless you're genuinely dead to your self and alive unto God. You will never use the authority that God's given you unless you're done with things being about you. You're not on this earth to be comfortable. You're on this earth to become love and manifest the image of God.

We need to get out of the way so the Holy Spirit can do what He wants with His bride.

Since I'm the gate of heaven, and because Jesus lives in me by the Spirit, then right now I'm seated next to my Father in heaven. It's my reality right now. That is where I'm at in the Spirit. I don't have to yell to get His attention. I just have to get still enough so I can hear His whisper to my heart.

So what's my reality when my health is in trouble? I go to the doctor, but I'm seated next to my Father at a higher reality in the Spirit.

Imagine that your kid's in trouble or your spouse is hooked on porn. Is that your reality? Or imagine that your lover has had an affair. Is that your reality? In the earthly realm, yes. But you are in a higher heavenly realm right now. You're at the feet of your Father. He's nearer than you would ever dream, and He will never leave you or forsake you. He promised.

When who you really are in Christ ceases to be your reality, you're on your own and you're trying to fight the battle that's already been won. When you forget where you are seated in Christ right now, on His throne with Him, then you'll likely fret and worry and get all worked up. And you will sin in your fear and doubt.

It Is Finished—Get in

Christians sometimes say to themselves, "I've got to try harder." That's about as dumb a thing as I've ever heard. "Try to be a better Christian." What's that all about?

Did Jesus say, "It is finished. Now you, Christian, finish what I already did"?

You don't have to "finish it" again. *It is finished!*

Many people will say, "If I could just pray more, if I could just fast more, if I could . . ." Well, if that's your attitude, it won't change anything. You can't really change anything except your response to God's grace and goodness.

Rather, our attitude should be, "If I could just fall deeper in love with Him . . ." If that's your attitude, it'll change everything. And it starts this way: "If I fall deeper in love with Jesus and get back to who I am seated in heavenly places with Jesus, then my mind won't block what God's trying to release through me into the world."

You have to die, Christian. You have to get in the casket. You have to lay yourself out and say, "I give up my life to you, Jesus."

There is no fear in death. Death is the last enemy. It's already been defeated. He just waits on us to give up our life.

Is your eye good today? Is it single? Seriously, is your eye single, or do you have options?

"But we believed God told us that person would live, and the person died. So I'm just a little leery."

No, we've got to die to circumstances because they don't change the truth. Jesus is truth, and Jesus is whom the Father speaks through now. We can't let circumstances speak louder than truth.

If we are offended or fearful, that means we picked up part of ourselves, and we're trying to do it and manage it ourselves. He wants us to give it all up and live "in the casket," so to speak, permanently "dead." He wants us to live in this state of reckless abandonment to His grace and His purposes. It's His truth.

Some say to me, "Dan, I'm not going to believe the way you believe."

Okay. You don't have to believe the way I believe, but you have to answer to God someday.

Others say to me, "I think that kind of faith is a bit too radical and sets people up for failure."

Well, where are we at now? How has that kind of thinking helped us?

I just believe. I'm not arrogant. I'm broken. I'm humble. But I believe.

I used to get hurt. I was so stupid. I would get hurt because people would talk about me. God convicted me of that. The Lord said to me, "You're hurt because of *that*?"

So if you want to talk about me and hurt me, go ahead. I'm not going to get mad and try to get even. I'm going to go home and weep over you and cry for you. And really, the worse you try to hurt me, the more likely you'll have an encounter with God because I don't want harm to come to you. I want you to meet Him. I am free to be this way because I'm dead.

The old me that used to get afraid when people talked about me, he died. I'm brand new. I'm so happy! I'm here to love you. And you can't change that.

I'm not writing this book for what you can do for me. I'm writing it to give you Jesus.

Why don't you just die to yourself? That's the route to freedom and joy in Jesus.

Some say, "Well, I've been hurt."

So was Jesus.

Others say, "I've been let down."

So was your Lord. He's already been through all that. You don't have to do it all over again. Let His finished work be finished in you.

If you want to lay down your life so that you're not in the way, and so God can use you for His glory, would you get on your knees right where you are and die? Come and die?

Right now.

PART 3

Faith Working Through Love

Jesus says, "If your eye is clear, your whole body will be full of light" (Matthew 6:22). Jesus is talking about clear vision, a singular focus. The best definition I could come up with is that Christ fills you with His presence. You're His house, His home, His temple. His eyes are looking through your eyes, and you're looking at life from His perspective, not yours.

We get in trouble when we look at the waves crashing on our lives instead of gazing at Him. He's the author and finisher of our faith. Anything is possible for those who believe. Do we believe that?

Galatians 5:6 says that the only thing that matters is faith working through love. Faith also casts out fear. So if you're in fear, you're not in faith. Faith is hearing the Word of God and doing whatever He says—no matter how long it takes, no matter how much it costs, and no matter how much it hurts. That's why in Mark 3 we see Jesus saying that His family is those who are sitting around Him, immovable, to the end. No matter how hard it gets, they don't leave Him. That's His family.

That's why in Luke 18:8 He says, "When the Son of Man comes, will He find faith on the earth?" He is saying, "Will I find people operating in loving faith and not fear?" Here's where we get into trouble. Our eyes are good. We have a fresh encounter with God. We feel His presence. Our vision is single. And then something distracts or derails us. Right? It may look like this: You believe the Word, you're living kingdom faith, and Christ is manifesting in your life. Then the doctor gives you a bad report. Here's the danger. We look with natural eyes and start thinking with the natural mind, and we get out of the mind of Christ. That's the problem.

When Some Are Not Healed and Others Are

My friend Bill is one of my closest friends and supporters. A couple years ago his son died of cancer. Directed by the Holy Spirit, I laid hands on that guy half a dozen times, and he still died. It ripped my heart out, and I got afraid.

I had been praying to the Lord, "God, of all the people that You should heal, definitely it needs to be Bill's son. Because Bill is one of my main supporters. He's a significant part of my ministry's power and security."

And you see the problem with all of this. It was all about "me and my" ministry. If it's about "me and my," then fear has a place to lodge every single time.

After Bill's son died, a year went by, and I found out his son's widow was diagnosed with stage four cancer.

Led by the Holy Spirit to conduct a healing service, I did so at the church where Bill attends, and Bill brought his widowed daughter-in-law because she wanted me to pray over her, even though I prayed for her husband and he died.

We have a choice every single day of our lives to eat from truth or the way "that seems right to man," the way of human knowledge or conventional human wisdom that makes sense to our natural mind.

So she was there in that service with stage four cancer. Bill invited her because the night before, some guy came to the service with stage four cancer; we prayed for him, and he said he was healed. He said when we touched him and prayed over him, he felt fire go through his belly where his cancer was.

Bill's daughter-in-law said, "I need to go have the church pray for me." Remember, her husband had died after we'd all prayed fervently for God to heal him. I started thinking about that with my natural mind. That's not a single-focus eye.

I said, "God, I don't know about this. I do not know what to do."

I clearly heard God say to me, "I want you to lay hands over her. I will heal her."

So she came walking up with her father-in-law, Bill. They stood there, and I put my hand on her, and she said I put my hand right where the tumor was. I didn't know where the tumor was. I didn't know anything about her, but she said she felt fire and electric currents go through her body. And later the doctors confirmed that her cancer was gone. Stage four cancer, gone. If I had kept my focus on what my natural eyes saw instead of what the spirit man was seeing, she probably would've died of cancer like her husband.

Every single one of us has that choice every single day to choose which tree we eat from. Every single one of us. Every single day.

I was once heading to California, and we stopped in Albuquerque and had a service where seven Nazarene churches and an Assembly of God church came together. The host pastor had stage four cancer all through his colon, all through his stomach. He was all gray. Near death.

I was looking at this pastor while I was preaching, but my heart would hardly let me preach because all I wanted was to see God touch this man. I prayed, "God, he loves You. He's all in. He's crying out."

God said to me, "I want you to call him up."

"What do you mean?"

"Call him up. I want you to touch him. I will heal him, and I want you to tell him he's healed."

The pastor couldn't walk. He was in a wheelchair because he was so sick from his chemo.

I said, "Come up here. God told me He wants to heal you."

So his wife pushed him to the front. I prayed for him, and God said to me, "That's not what I said. You need to tell him the cancer's gone."

"Huh?" I said to the Lord, "Look, God, he has stage four cancer all the way through his stomach and intestines. It's everywhere." What I saw with my natural eye made my natural mind think that way. Why would I say, "It's gone when it's not gone yet?"

The Spirit said, "Tell him."

I said, "Paul, I don't know how to say this because you don't look good right now. But the Spirit of God inside me told me to tell you that the cancer's gone, so you don't have to worry about it." His wife started crying. He just looked sicker.

So we finished, and I went on my trip to six churches in California. I didn't know if the pastor had been healed or not. I just knew I heard from the Spirit of God and that I had obeyed Him in telling the pastor what I told him.

When I was at my dear friend's church in California, we were praying for a pastor's young son who was put in a coma more than eight years earlier by a medical accident. He was partially paralyzed and needed twenty-four-hour medical care. He was brought to the healing service, and he didn't get healed.

I said, "God, I believed You were going to heal him. Why did he not get healed?"

God said, "Look at that! Look at what is going on right next to him."

There was another young man, twenty-three-years-old with cerebral palsy. His legs were all bent up. He'd spent all of his life in a wheelchair.

The Lord said to me, "I want you to pray for that young man."

Now I had a choice. Every single day of your life you have the choice before you. You can eat from the tree of life, that is, to believe truth. The Word of God's truth says that you "will lay hands on the sick, and they will recover" (Mark 16:18). Or you can eat of the tree that says, "Well, God doesn't always heal everybody." That's the tree of human knowledge and reasoning.

We say things like, "We're going through this season. He's teaching me lessons through this pain." I won't argue that, but we make up all kinds of stuff that Jesus didn't operate in. And we make it up because it seems reasonable. It sounds like wisdom because it comes from a voice that almost sounds like truth. But it's twisted.

I said to my friend the pastor, "Tell me this guy's story."

So the pastor told me, "He's been in my church all of his life. He's the only guy who comes to the altar when I invite people forward to deal with God. Every single altar call, he wheels his motorized wheelchair up to the altar. He is about the only person who ever comes forward."

I thought, "Great. He has cerebral palsy. He's never walked."

I turned to him. "Do you want to walk?"

He goes, "Yeah!"

I put my hands on him and prayed. He got up and started walking.

The pastor's son didn't get up. This young man with cerebral palsy did. Same service. I don't understand why the one young man didn't get up, but I'm not going to get offended at God.

I don't know what's missing in my faith because Jesus could get him up just like that. We set up hierarchies in degrees of miracles, degrees of difficulty, because we give cancer a greater authority than we give a broken back or a cold.

Why is that? Because we base our paradigms of faith on our experiences and our circumstances instead of Jesus' experience in His circumstance.

So we were driving back from California, and the stage-four-cancer pastor in Albuquerque posted on my Facebook page, "Just got back from my CT scan. MRI. No cancer."

Was it easy in that service to tell him God had healed him? Or was it the scariest thing I'd ever said? When God tells you to do something, it usually makes no sense to the natural mind.

So you can have a single-eye focus, and your whole body will be influenced by truth, or you can have a divided eye, and the light inside you will be dark. When we do that, our whole perspective gets twisted so that we believe God enough to get to heaven, but we don't really believe we can do and experience what He said we can now. So we put limitations on what the power of the gospel can do in our lives.

Knowing the Holy Spirit

A while back, the Holy Spirit convicted me that I didn't know Him the way He wanted me to know Him.

I said, "How do I get to know the Holy Spirit better?"

He said, "Start by studying Jesus' last night's teachings before He went to the cross. That's the best way to get to know who the Holy Spirit is."

In the upper room on the night that Jesus is arrested, He teaches extensively on the Holy Spirit.

John the Apostle was probably Jesus' closest, intimate friend. God gave John the revelation to write down Jesus' last words before He went to the cross. Because John was so intimate with Jesus, he got the greater revelation.

The Holy Spirit told me to study John chapters 13–17 because this is "the farewell discourse of Jesus." He is sharing His most intimate words with His disciples before He goes to die for our sins. He is excited to share with them about the Holy Spirit.

John is "the one whom Jesus loved." That is, the one who is in Jesus' heart, the one most intimate with Jesus. So John gets all this revelation from God about this night because he operates out of the heart of Jesus' life.

In John 13:3 we read that Jesus knew "that the Father had given all things into His hands, and that He had come forth from God and was going back to God." This verse tells us that Jesus knew who He was, where He was from, and where He was going. He had His identity clear. And because of that He could take off His robe and get low and vulnerable and wash feet.

John 13:4–5 tell us He "got up from supper, and laid aside His garments; and taking a towel, He girded Himself. Then He poured water into the basin, and began to wash the disciples' feet and to wipe them with the towel with which He was girded."

Peter says, "You're not washing my feet."

Sounds like a lot of Christians. "I'm already saved and sanctified. You don't need to wash my feet. I took a bath before I came to church."

Jesus says to Peter, "If I don't wash you, you have no part in Me."

So Peter responds with a carnal mind, "Lord, then wash not my feet only, but also my hands and my head" (13:9). In other words, "I want You to do it the way I want it done."

Jesus essentially says, "I don't have your idea in My plan. It's My idea or no idea. I have a way. It is the only way."

But we say things like, "Don't get your hopes up. You'll just get hurt." Where does that come from? Hope is the whole foundation for the gospel. Hope doesn't disappoint us.

I've had people say to me, "Would you pray for this person? They are always pushing my wrong buttons, and they're really irritating me."

I'd rather pray, "Lord, get rid of her buttons."

People come to me and say, "Can you just pray, man? This person is getting under my skin."

You know what? Get rid of your skin!

People ask me, "Can you pray that I get a new job? I work around all these people who aren't Christians."

I can't pray that prayer. I want you to let your light shine so brightly that all those people who aren't Christians *become* Christians because you're working there. I can't pray prayers that God doesn't want to answer.

So on that fateful night in the upper room, Peter says to Jesus, "Do it my way." Jesus says, "No."

Then Jesus says, "I've set an example, and all of you need to follow Me."

In John 13:15 He says, "One of you is going to betray me."

Peter asks, "Who's going to do it?"

"The one I give the bread to."

Who's the one He gives the bread to? Judas. Judas is His friend. And he's about to betray Jesus.

But Jesus is love, and love never fails. Love doesn't keep a record of wrongs, try to get even, or try to manipulate. It just focuses its affection on the highest objective. When God looks at us, His highest objective is that we become like Him.

So Judas leaves the upper room and betrays Jesus. And Peter says, "I'll never leave you. I mean, I'm never going to leave." Jesus doesn't even respond to Peter.

Then Jesus says something that bothers me. It bothers me because we don't do it. "A new commandment I give to you, that you love one another, even as I have loved you, that you also love one another. By this all men will know that you are My disciples, if you have love for one another" (John 13:34–35).

The phrase "even as" in verse 34 is the Greek word *kathos*. It means "exactly the same way."

"Jesus, do you mean my enemies? Do you mean I have to bless my enemies and love them the way You love me and the way You loved and blessed Your enemies? You put the ear back on the guy who was trying to arrest You. You forgave the guys nailing you to the cross while they were doing it. Really?"

That's exactly what Jesus is saying.

That's what we miss. We are holiness people. We believe that Jesus' blood sets us free from sin. Yet in Matthew 6 where Jesus models prayer, He says that when you pray, ask God to forgive you of your sins. Why would we have to ask God to forgive us of our sins if we're not sinning? Maybe because we're not loving people the way Jesus loved us. And that's a form of sin.

Jesus' Kind of Love

I can love my friends. I would die for my grandkids. I'd take a bullet for my wife. But an enemy? Jesus laid His life down for all of us, including His enemies. He didn't have any friends when He laid His life down. The Bible says that we were all His enemies when He died for us. Listen to Romans 5:6–10.

> *For while we were still helpless, at the right time Christ died for the ungodly. For one will hardly die for a righteous man; though perhaps for the good man someone would dare even to die. But God demonstrates His own love toward us, in that while we were yet sinners, Christ died for us. Much more then, having now been justified by His blood, we shall be saved from the wrath of God through Him. For if while we were enemies we were reconciled to God through the death of His Son, much more, having been reconciled, we shall be saved by His life.*

Note the words that God inspired the apostle Paul to write in this passage to describe us when Jesus died for us: "helpless," "ungodly," "sinners," "enemies." And yet God demonstrates His love toward us when we were still sinners and His enemies.

That's how Jesus is saying that we're supposed to love people. That's why we must not judge people according to the flesh.

Too often we get all bent out of shape, and we get hurt and say things like, "Ministry would be great if it weren't for the people." We say things like that because we let what they are in the flesh rule what we see. Rather, we should see in the Spirit the way Jesus sees.

Sometimes Christians say things like, "That person prayed, and God forgave him when he was on crack, and he got delivered. But now he's back on crack, and he doesn't come to church anymore."

That's not your problem. It's between him and God.

"This other person got delivered from pornography and then after that had an affair."

That's between them and God. You did what you're supposed to do.

In Luke 24:47 Jesus says, "Repentance for forgiveness of sins would be proclaimed in His name to all the nations, beginning from Jerusalem." Repentance and remission of sins. Repentance is what we do. It means "to change your mind." We live repentant lifestyles when we continually change our minds and our actions to agree with God and line up with His Word. We live lives where we don't want anything to come between God and us. We want to keep turning and looking to Jesus, the author and perfecter of our faith.

So repentance isn't only repenting for your sins, repentance is also changing your mind, changing your perspective, and getting a better vision of Jesus. It's thinking differently. It's setting your mind on things above. It's believing the truth that what He did was enough. We don't have to add to it.

But what about remission? What is remission? It's not just forgiveness. It's a word that means that He not only forgives our sins, He also removes the cause and the effect of what sin brought into our life to begin with, as if it never happened.

Sin brought all this junk in that we deal with, and we call it normal because it's the way "that seems right to man" because we have science to back it up.

I read a 980-page book about John G. Lake. He was a mighty man of God whom the Lord used in incredible ways in South Africa. All these Red Cross people showed up because the bubonic plague had swept the nation, and everybody was dying. Lake was burying the bodies, and he didn't have on a mask or anything. Many days his clothes would be completely soaked with the body fluids of the dead and dying. The Red Cross was so afraid of catching the plague that they wouldn't even come ashore. They couldn't believe that John G. Lake was surviving and not getting the plague. They asked him, "What are you doing?" He said, "The Spirit of life has set me free from the spirit of death and sin." That was His reality. And the plague never touched him.

Many would say, "That guy's out of His mind." Good. I think he was so heavenly minded that he no longer lived by "what seems right to man." You can be out of your earthly mind because of Jesus.

Jesus not only forgave our sins, but He took away all the cause and effects of sin. If we really believe God's Word when it says that we're saved through the sanctifying work of the Spirit, then everything changes.

What does the sanctifying work of the Spirit do? It preserves your spirit, soul, and body. It touches your spiritual being, your emotional being, and your physical being. That's the gospel. That's why Paul says in Romans 1:16, "I'm not ashamed of the gospel because it's the power [dunamis in Greek] of God unto salvation [soteria in Greek]." And the word soteria can mean to preserve, to be made whole, to be delivered, to be set free, to be healed, to be forgiven, to be cleansed. We just call it "forgiveness" or "salvation."

Soteria means so much more than just forgiveness or what we think of when we say the word "salvation." It means more than forgiveness or your name written in a book in heaven. It means that everything's been made new and all the old is gone. That is, if you really believe it.

When you read the Bible, you find a bunch of curses on people because of sin. And Jesus wiped the slate of sin clean. He paid all the debts. All the curses are removed, and He paid every debt that you couldn't pay, except for one. That debt is mentioned in Romans 13:8. It is the ongoing debt of love that we owe to everybody.

In John 13:34 Jesus tells us that He is giving us "a new commandment." The word for "new" here is the word *kainos* in Greek. It means something that's not been seen or heard before. It's new because nobody's been doing it.

So on His last night before He gets arrested, Jesus gives us His new commandment. Essentially He says, "I'm saving my best words for last. And I'm going to tell you the best part of what I'm about and what you're getting ready to be about. And this is right at the heart of it. You have to love people just as I have loved you."

Remember, Jesus' kind of love can never fail.

At that point Peter pipes up. "Jesus, I don't care if everybody leaves you. I'll die for you!" Then at the end of John 13, Jesus says, "Will you really lay down your life for me?" Jesus knows Peter and He knows the future. "A rooster will not crow until you have denied Me three times." Yet Jesus still loves Peter and still wants Peter to be on His team. Can you believe such love?

The question that Jesus asks Peter that night is the question He poses to every one of us who follow: "Will you deny yourself, take up your cross, and lay down your life for me?"

Jesus didn't say, "Will you come and say a prayer? Come, say a prayer so you can get your name in a book in heaven so that you can go there someday."

The question Jesus asks all of us is, "Will you really lay down your life for me?"

John 13 is the pattern. It's a pattern of what *agape* love looks like. Jesus' kind of love (*agape* in Greek) goes low. It is the love of a humble servant. The Son of Man didn't come to be served. He came to serve. He came to give His life as a ransom for many. And Jesus says to all of us, "Now, you follow after Me. Walk in My steps. Do what I do."

John 13 is the chapter where Jesus lovingly washes His guys' feet. Jesus shows us how love looks. It serves. It cares. It forgives. That's our pattern.

Jesus' Dwelling

In John 14:1, while Jesus and His disciples are still in the upper room, Jesus turns to His disciples and says, "Do not let your heart be troubled; believe in God, believe also in Me." When, like the disciples, we feel "troubled" or "disturbed," or "stirred up," we easily and naturally vacillate or feel torn between two ideas or views. For example, part of the disciples' minds believes the truth, the kingdom of God, and that Jesus is the Son of God. Part of them still worries about the Romans. Their minds are torn between two opinions.

Part of us still worries about our job and part of us still worries about the way that seems right to man. We must not let our mind be torn between two identities. Believe in Jesus regardless of circumstances.

Then Jesus says, "In my Father's house are many dwelling places; if it were not so, I would have told you; for I go to prepare a place for you. If I go and prepare a place for you, I will come again and receive you to Myself, that where I am, there you may be also" (John 14:2–3). We have room reservations in heaven! Nothing and no one can cancel them. So take lifelong hope and anticipation of your destination.

Well, what about right now?

We get a clue in John 1:14. "And the Word became flesh, and dwelt among us."

The word "dwelt" doesn't mean "lived" or "took up residence." It has a far greater meaning. The Greek root word is *skene* (sounds like "skaynay"), and it means "tabernacle." The verse literally says that Jesus took human form and "tabernacled" (*eskenosen*) among us. He became a living, breathing, two-legged tabernacle of God.

Then at Pentecost the privilege is extended to all humanity. When the Spirit is poured out, we can all become tabernacles, or temples. Paul affirms this twice—in 1 Corinthians 3:16, "Do you not know that you are a temple of God and that the Spirit of God dwells in you?" And 6:19 says, "Do you not know that your body is a temple of the Holy Spirit who is in you, whom you have from God, and that you are not your own?"

We are God's temples. Our physical bodies are His temples. His Spirit dwells inside us. You can't get more intimate than that. You can't even get that intimate with your loving spouse. They don't live inside you the way God's Holy Spirit does.

The disciples will soon—after the cross, resurrection, and ascension—have that intimacy. You and I have that intimacy. We have it now. Each of us is God's temple, His intimate dwelling place here on earth.

And Jesus is going to prepare a heavenly dwelling place for us all. The address of that dwelling place is in God's heavenly territory, not on earth. Imagine how much more intimate we'll be with God then. It just gets better and better!

In John 14:3 when Jesus says, "I will come again and receive you to myself," the word "receive" means more than just "accept." It's a bringing together. In line with His prayer in John 17, Jesus is saying, "We will merge together. We will become one together, where we won't be able to tell where you end and I begin. We will be one as the Father and I are one, so that everywhere I go, you'll go. Everything I see, you'll see. Every person I touch, I'll use your fingers. Everything I say, I'll use your heart, your mind, your personality, and your mouth."

Then Jesus says, "You know the way where I am going" (John 14:4). The disciples are now saying, "What is He talking about?"

And that sounds like most of the church today. God wants to tell us so much, but too many of us can't handle it yet.

It's like what Jesus said earlier in His ministry, when He said in essence, "I don't want to put condemnation on you, so I'll just keep telling you parables because you're held liable for what you know. And if you don't know much, maybe you have a chance that grace gets in before you know too much. I'd like to share my deepest secrets with you, but so many of you only want fire insurance from hellfire. You don't really want to be intimate with Me as My bride."

And then Jesus says this, "I'm the Way. I'm the Truth. I'm the Life." He is the way to the Father in heaven that no one else could ever be. Isn't that good news?

Then Jesus puts one of those statements in. It's kind of like a stinger. He says, "If you had known Me, you would have known My Father also; from now on you know Him, and have seen Him" (John 14:7). Jesus is saying, "If you had truly known who I am, you would already have known who My Father is."

Then in John 14:10 Jesus makes one of the great statements of the Bible, "Do you not believe that I am in the Father, and the Father is in Me? The words that I say to you I do not speak on My own initiative, but the Father abiding in Me does His works."

Jesus is saying, "It's not My words. It's the Father's words, and it is His authority doing these things."

John 14:10 is a pattern of what a Spirit-filled Christian should be. That is, living life not on our ideas and our own impulses, but on every impulse and every heartthrob of the Father that can't wait to be released through us.

And if you think that's wild, John 14:11 basically says, "Guys, believe that I'm in My Father, and He's in me. But if you have a hard time with that, look at the miracles I'm doing."

So many people erroneously think that Jesus did the miracles, healings, and signs and wonders simply because He was God. And they say, "Well, that's God. It was easy for Him because He was God."

Yes, He was God incarnate. But when performing miracles, that's not what He relied on. Jesus relied on the Holy Spirit to flow through Him at all times. So the miracles happened because they were the authority of God, not Jesus Himself. He relied on the Holy Spirit just as He wants us to rely on the Holy Spirit.

He says, "I preached to you guys for three years. You're not getting it. Look at the miracles that are happening through Me. How many sermons does it take before you get it?"

Why do you think Paul says in 1 Corinthians 2, "You guys need to get your eyes off of good, eloquent speakers and quit letting your faith rest on the guy who sounds like the three points of his sermon match the best. You need to get your faith on a demonstration of the power of the Spirit."

How many sermon series does it take for you to become love? It just takes your being willing to go to the cross and die so Christ can live His life through you.

Acts 1:8 says, "You will receive power when the Holy Spirit has come upon you; and you shall be My witnesses both in Jerusalem, and in all Judea and Samaria, and even to the remotest part of the earth."

You'll receive power. Power from on high. When the Holy Spirit gets all of you, you'll receive power, and you'll be witnesses unto God. What does that verse really mean?

What does the first part of Acts 1:8 really mean? If you break it down grammatically, it means that if the Holy Spirit gets all of you, and He has access to flow through you the way He wants to, He'll start doing things through you that there's no way you'll get credit for it because people will look at you and say, "I know you couldn't pull that off. It must be God inside you doing that."

Your life will bring witness unto God. People will look at you and see that 2 Corinthians 4:7 is true: God's great power lives in earthen vessels. You're just a cracked pot, a weak earthen vessel. There must be glory in you somewhere because you couldn't pull this off.

Then there's Romans 15:16 where Paul says that he wants to be a minister of the gospel and present people as an offering acceptable to God because they've been sanctified by the Holy Spirit. Verse 19 continues in saying that God confirms the message with signs and wonders. He is teaching that supernatural signs and wonders accompany the true message of the gospel, and they fulfill the gospel—the same gospel you and I believe.

Being Weak to Be Strong

I read a book by a Harvard professor who's an atheist trying to disprove Christianity. He studied the first hundred years from Acts 2 onward. He reported that for the first two and a half generations of Christians, the Church of Jesus Christ didn't have any infrastructure. They didn't have any district superintendents. They didn't have any general superintendents. They didn't have any money. They had no Bible schools. They didn't have anything except power. They had the supernatural power of God on them that Jesus had prophesied they would have when the Holy Spirit came upon them. They didn't have a denominational name. They were simply the people who looked like Jesus, acted like Jesus, and loved like Jesus—and they were called Christians.

This atheist professor says the only thing they had in common was a power flowing through them that nobody else could stop. It brought witness to God. And the more they were persecuted, the more they multiplied.

Too many of us say, "I can't get anybody to pray." And we wonder, "Are they ever going to get it?"

Can you see Peter and Paul wringing their hands at the prayer meeting and whining to the Lord, "God, you know, we need resources, we need air conditioning. It's going to be hard to keep the kids here during the summer if we don't have air conditioning. Give us some ideas. You know, Lord, Nero's coming down on us pretty hard. And this homosexual thing's getting out of hand."

No, they just prayed, "Lord, stretch forth your hand. Do more miracles!"

So many so-called Christians are comfortable not reading the Bible. But if you open it up and take it seriously, be careful because it's a dangerous book. It will yank you out of everything you thought was normal. It will challenge your paradigms and your thinking patterns. You will never be the same.

So Jesus says, "If you guys don't get it because of my preaching, look at the miracles. I'm one of you. The Holy Spirit is flowing into Me the same way He will flow through you if you let Him."

God says in Corinthians 12:9, "My grace is sufficient for you, for power is perfected in weakness." And Paul affirms in verse 10, "When I am weak, then I am strong."

If we're willing to become weaker and weaker, there's no end to His strength. The moment we think we can do without Him and we press our will, it diminishes His power, and there's a ceiling on what we can accomplish. But if we're willing to stay weak and dependent and poor in spirit, the whole kingdom keeps pouring out on us. The power of God keeps tabernacling with us. If we keep on being honest in our weakness, then His strength has a place to be made complete and perfect.

God's power was perfected in Jesus' demonstration of weakness on the cross. Jesus always stayed dependent on His Father's Word and love.

If we'll stay poor in spirit, God's power can flow through us. There's no end to His upside, and it'll continually give witness to God. People will look at you and me, and they'll say, "I know you, and there's no way you could pull this off. It has to be God in you."

The harder your situation, or the more desperate and hopeless you feel—that's where healing and cleansing can burst out of nowhere, and God will get all the glory when you least expect it.

When Jesus died on the cross, His healing was released to mankind. Though physically strong, you could say that He was the weakest human there ever was because He had more to give up than any of us could fathom. And when he became weak, the power of God burst out of His death.

Doing Greater Things

Now we come to one of the greatest things Jesus ever said: "Truly, truly, I say to you, he who believes in Me, the works that I do, he will do also; and greater works than these he will do; because I go to the Father" (John 14:12). This is one of the most unbelievable utterances that Jesus ever made. Most born-again Christians do not believe this verse. Jesus is saying that if we believe in Him, He expects us to do the very same signs, wonders, miracles, deliverances, exorcisms, and healings that He did—and even greater works than He did.

Some say, "Well, that was for the twelve."

Where's that in the Bible?

Jesus said that as His disciple makers, we are supposed to teach our own disciples to do everything He taught (Matthew 28:20). That would include the truth of John 14:12—that the disciples of Jesus will do "greater works" than Jesus did.

When I don't see a problem with my natural eyes, I have greater faith to believe for the miraculous. For example, when I don't see the actual physical condition of the person I'm praying for, I seem to have greater faith for their healing. Over the phone or over Facebook, I receive more testimonies of miracles than I do in the services.

I think this is because what I'm seeing with my natural eyes is not affecting my natural mind when I'm doing it over the phone or over the internet. It's when I'm in the hospital room and I see the pitiful condition of the sick person that my faith dwindles because my natural mind starts building paradigms that are contrary to the promises of God. And I'll think, "Maybe God is not going to do it this time."

When I do that, it's all based on what I see instead of what I don't see. And I haven't learned to be like Jesus yet where He could see a person on a mat and say, "Get up!" And it didn't matter if the sick person was on the mat or not. He just got up.

I have a pastor friend in Detroit. He called me and said His wife was on life support and she was dying. Would I pray? Of course I would. I had great faith on the phone. I'm not in the ICU with her, seeing deathly condition. So I pray with faith, "Lord, resurrect her! Bring her back!" And the next morning she came back from the dead.

She testified that she found herself in a tunnel. She saw a light. Then she felt something grab her back. At the very time we were praying on the phone, she sat up in her bed. They took the breathing tube out, and she went home that night. They couldn't explain it.

I don't know if I would have had the faith to do that if I had been in the room with her.

But what if my reality were, "I am the room the Holy Spirit lives in"? "I *can* do all things through Christ who strengthens me."

Here's another instance.

I was at Nampa, Idaho, First Church of the Nazarene, and it's a big church. I was preaching on the kind of faith that amazes God. In the middle of my sermon, a very old lady, all bent over, came walking up with a cane, all the way to the front. And she stopped right in front of me. In front of the whole congregation. While I was preaching.

I looked at her and said, "Yes?" But I was thinking, "What kind of audacity is this? She walks right in front of me. While I'm preaching."

She said, "I'm in pain. I need to be healed."

"How old are you?"

"I'm ninety."

I thought in my heart, "What do you expect?" That's probably what you would have thought too.

Then I said it. "Well, what do you expect?" And all of a sudden my single vision went out the window, and I was thinking, "You've got to be kidding me. She's not taking my message serious. She's ninety. This is for people under forty."

The Holy Spirit whispered to me, "Heal her." So I put my hands on her and prayed.

She turned around, she took two steps and threw her cane down and stood up all the way upright all the way back to her seat.

She kept saying out loud, "The pain's gone, the pain's gone, the pain's gone!" It was Daniel Ketchum's mother.

There was another instance. A little lady came up to me with a baby in her arms. "Can I testify?"

I said, "Yeah."

"When you were here last year, I asked you to pray for my feet. I was scheduled to have an abortion on the following day. You prayed for my feet. There hadn't been a heartbeat of my baby for three weeks, and my baby was dead inside me. And so they were going to do an abortion the next day to take my dead baby out." Then she held up the baby in her arms. "This is the thirteen-month-old baby."

I had prayed for her feet. God raised her baby from the dead that I hadn't even prayed for.

I don't think I would have had faith if I could have seen a dead baby. I'm trying to say that sometimes the only way you can see by faith is to not look with the natural eyes.

You've got to see with His eyes. Jesus said that we will do what He did, and even greater things, because He was going to the Father.

Doing Anything

Then Jesus says, "You can ask anything in my name, and I'll do it" (John 14:13–14). Now the word "ask" is really a word that might better be interpreted "declare." It's not a word for beg, plead, or yearn. It's to declare.

In other words, you know what's going to happen because you live under God's authority and leading. You're seeing your problem from God's vantage point, and you're praying from God's perspective, not yours. You're not praying from your problem. You're praying from the right hand of the Father, from His promises, and from His perspective. You are close enough to Him that He has told you what He is about to do. You know that nothing's too hard for Him, so you can just declare what He's getting ready to do.

It's like what Peter says in Acts 2, that the pouring out of the Spirit was what the prophet Joel spoke of—and it was happening. Peter doesn't say, "God, pour out your Spirit. He just declares, "This is what's happening."

Who would have the audacity to declare things? Only the people who are operating cheek to cheek with God. If we're trying to do it on our own, it's hit and miss.

Then Jesus says in John 14:15, "If you love Me, you will keep My commandments." *Tereo* is the word Jesus used here for the word "keep." It can be used in the sense of "you'll build this wall of protection around My commands."

Everything God commands you to do is not just for you. It's also what He wants to do through you to change the world around you because you're not a person with a bunch of problems anymore. You're the person now who is Jesus' answer and has answers because Jesus lives in you.

James 1:22 says, "Prove yourselves doers of the word, and not merely hearers who delude yourselves." The word "doers" is *poietes*. And it means to carry out one's given task or even perform one's script. So don't just sit around critiquing messages and saying you're not being fed, then going to the next church. Carry out the task or perform the script that God has given you to live out in that church.

So often we hear things like, "I wasn't getting fed in that church. They didn't meet my needs. It just wasn't right. Nobody said hi to me last Sunday. Nobody shook my hands. I didn't get invited out with the pastor."

When did church become all about meeting our needs?

If you are love, if the Spirit of God lives in you, then the whole church should have been feeling loved the day you were there. If you walked in the place and you're full of God, everyone you interact with should feel loved.

When did the church become all about you? When did it become about your being fed? What about *your* feeding the sheep? We shouldn't come to church, saying, "Gimme, gimme." We should come to church, saying and praying, "Make me more like You, Jesus, so You can flow through me."

Jesus never got hurt because of what people said or did, but He hurt *for* those people. Jesus wept over people because He hurt for them. But they couldn't hurt Him because he was love, and love is not "hurtable."

You know why you're hurtable? Because there are still things you hold on to. Or because you have taken up things again that you once gave over to Jesus.

Persevering is not simply digging in and holding on. Persevering is falling in love with Jesus no matter how hard it gets. What would it be like if every person reading this book were willing to sink out of sight as Jesus did, trusting ourselves to our Abba Father?

Every one of us could ask God for anything, and He would be happy to answer our prayers because they start from Him, He would get all the glory because of our heart's posture.

We're on the verge, aren't we? What's your heart telling you? Is there pride? Is there fear? Wouldn't it be nice if all that was destroyed, and we could just experience the power of God?

We have our mission.

How in the world do we get so hurt if we're becoming love? It's because we replace intimacy and relationship with Jesus for religious duties and practices, and then we get offended and hurt when Jesus doesn't answer us. But He's saying, "I'm still waiting on you to come and become intimate with Me."

Maybe you've allowed some callouses to come into your life. Or maybe you've allowed yourself to become "hurtable."

Would you be willing to lay your life down and give your best gift to God? Would you do that right where you are right now?

Would you say, "God, I surrender. I give up. I give my life to you. I don't want to hold on to anything or hold anything back."

We don't have to wait for a breakthrough. It's already happened. The stone has been rolled away. We have a breakthrough.

We just need to let it be our reality.

PART 4

Hearing and Doing

Hebrews 11:6 says that God rewards those who diligently seek Him. I think His rewards are worth diligently seeking, but before we do that, we need to listen.

Let's look at John 15:22–24. "If I had not come and spoken to them, they would not have sin, but now they have no excuse for their sin. He who hates Me hates My Father also. If I had not done among them the works which no one else did, they would not have sin; but now they have both seen and hated Me and My Father as well."

When we look closely at Jesus' life and ministry, we see an interesting pattern. Many times Jesus speaks before He does anything.

That's why we have to be intimate enough with Him and close enough to Him to hear what He is saying. This way we'll know what He's about to do.

Jesus Says It, then He Does It

In 1995 I was driving to work and got hit by a semi truck. I spent thirteen months in a hospital bed. When the semi hit me, it broke my back, broke my pelvis, tore my liver, and tore the urethra out of my bladder. I had to have surgeries on my organs, and I was soon to have surgeries on my back and pelvis to rebuild them. One night, after the surgeries on my organs and before the surgeries on my back and pelvis, I was lying in my bed, and the Holy Spirit said, "By the way, I can heal your body. Just reach out and touch me."

He spoke to me, but He didn't heal me until I believed it.

It was two in the morning. The Holy Spirit said to me, "I can heal your body. I've taken care of your family. I've healed your spirit. I've provided for your needs. You can't work. You can't walk. You're just lying here in this bed, reading My book."

Then he said, "I can heal your body too. Just reach out. Touch me."

So I raised my arms, and tingles and fire went down both arms. The tingles and fire went down my body all the way to my feet. I was instantly healed, and they never had to do surgery on my pelvis or my back. Praise God Almighty!

You can't talk me out of what I believe. You'll just get mad trying to, so do yourself a favor and don't bother.

People come to me and say, "Well, you don't understand."

I don't have to understand because you can't talk me out of it, because I've seen it and experienced it. When God heals you like that, you become a very convinced believer.

I haven't just heard it and read about it. Jesus says it and then He does it. That's His usual pattern.

And He tells us in John 15:26, "When the Helper comes, whom I will send to you from the Father, that is the Spirit of truth who proceeds from the Father, He will testify about Me." In 16:1 He goes on to say, "These things I have spoken to you so that you may be kept from stumbling." The Greek word for "stumbling" is *skandalizo*, which means to cause someone to sin or give up their faith. The English world "scandalous" comes from it. So Jesus is saying, "The whole reason I'm speaking to you is to help keep you from sinning or losing faith."

In essence, Jesus is saying to His most devoted men, "The reason I'm telling you all of this is because if you really start living My life and become love, and realize you're the dwelling place of My Spirit, that changes everything. When you guys realize that you're the channel My kingdom flows through, it will totally change you. If you start living this, people are not going to like you. The reason I'm teaching you this is so you'll have fortitude to endure to the end. If you get religious and political, you'll get promoted and have a good financial package. But if you truly follow Me and let Me live through you by the power of the Spirit, then you will have troubles, and I don't want you to stumble when the opposition comes."

Jesus goes on to say in John 16:2, "They will make you outcasts from the synagogue, but an hour is coming for everyone who kills you to think that he is offering service to God."

Jesus says that they will be excommunicated from the synagogue, the Jewish gathering for worship, which is similar to the Greek *ekklesia*, the Christian gathering for worship. Who are the people that are going to be excommunicated? The people who are living the life of Jesus. And people who literally kill these believers will actually think that God is pleased with them.

Who in the world would think or act this way? In the context of what Jesus is saying, it's those who are in charge of organized religion.

Think about that.

Jesus explains why: "These things they will do because they have not known the Father or Me" (16:3). The religious leaders do not truly know God or His Son Jesus. So they misunderstand and oppose those who do.

Then Jesus tells them, "Now I am going to Him who sent Me; and none of you asks Me, 'Where are You going?' But because I have said these things to you, sorrow has filled your heart. But I tell you the truth, it is to your advantage that I go away; for if I do not go away, the Helper will not come to you; but if I go, I will send Him to you" (John 16:5–7).

How can Jesus' going away be to our *advantage*? Jesus is essentially saying, "Physically, I can only be one place at one time. But if I go back to heaven and send My Spirit to you all, everything I do could start happening through all of my people."

So all at the same time, somebody might get born again; somebody else might get healed of cancer; another may get healed of depression; somebody's marriage may be restored—all over the world. Jesus knows this can only happen if He goes away. Although we will miss Him, the result is to our advantage.

Soon after Jesus' ascension, this advantage happened in Acts 2. While believers are seeking God, the heavens tear open, and the glory of God's presence fills the room. The Spirit comes upon each one of them, manifesting in the appearance of fire over each person. And each person speaks by the leading of the Holy Spirit in the many languages represented by the people there.

Jesus goes on to say that the Holy Spirit will convict the world of the sin of unbelief, of Christ's righteousness, and of judgment on Satan. Then in 16:12, after three years of being with his eleven closest friends, He tells them, "I still have many things to say to you, but you can't bear them yet."

Don't you want to be a person that He can tell anything to?

Look at what Jesus says next on that fateful night in the upper room. "But when He, the Spirit of truth, comes, He will guide you into all the truth; for He will not speak on His own initiative, but whatever He hears, He will speak; and He will disclose to you what is to come" (John 16:13).

Even the Holy Spirit only speaks what He hears from the Father in heaven. Then in turn the Holy Spirit intends to guide us past the basics, past many of the things we tend to get tangled in, and into the limitless possibilities that are ours in the kingdom of God. Jesus' Spirit will become our tour guide into all our tomorrows. I had a guide in the Holy Land who knew all about the Holy Land and all about the Bible, but she couldn't see Jesus. The Holy Spirit, on the other hand, will guide us to faith and into the mysteries of God. He tells us, then he does it.

Hearing and Responding

I was at a church in Nebraska, and at the end of one service, I asked, "Who needs a breakthrough? Who needs a miracle?" About fifty people came to the front.

I didn't know where to start. "Lord, who do I pray with?" There were too many. As I paused and listened, He directed me to go to a certain lady. I asked God, "What do You want me to pray for this lady?"

Don't you hate it when you ask somebody to pray, and they just start praying what they want? Usually nothing happens. Wouldn't it be amazingly different if we would pray only after we take the time to listen to Him and find out how *He* wants us to pray? How could we do that unless we first hear Him speak before we start praying? We need to listen more before we just start speaking in prayer.

So as I was looking at this lady, the Holy Spirit said, "Tell her that you know she's been really hurt by people in the church, and I want to heal her heart so she can embrace what I'm doing in the church again—and feel part of it."

I said, "Are you sure?"

He said to my heart, "Yes."

So I simply said that to her, and the next day her husband came in smiling.

"What's going on?" I asked.

He handed me a $10,000 check.

"What's that for?"

"My wife's never been so happy in all of her life. Everything you said to her last night was what she's been dealing with. How did you know that?"

"I don't know anything." I just said what the Holy Spirit told me to say.

I wonder if God wants to pour resources through all of us to change our cities so they become outposts of the kingdom? He has to tell somebody what He wants to do. Can it be you?

Another time I was in Indiana, and I was praying, waiting on the Lord, and not really feeling much spiritually.

Aren't you glad it's not about feelings?

As I sat in the presence of the Lord, the Holy Spirit said, "Why you don't care that I like your wife's desires as much as I like your desires?"

"What are You talking about? I do everything I can to take care of my wife."

The Holy Spirit said, "Calm down."

Isn't it funny how we can get offended when God's trying to teach us something? That happens because we think we have rights.

If we truly died to ourselves in coming to faith, how can we think we have rights? How can we get offended if we're dead?

So I said, "What do you mean, God?"

"Your wife's been wanting an RV for five years, and you keep blowing her off, thinking it's not important. What if it's important to Me that your wife wants it, and I want to give it to her?"

"Well, I'm not buying an RV. I don't have any money."

"I didn't say you had to buy one. Why don't you think I care about your wife?"

I said, "I believe you care about my wife. If you want us to have an RV, it's okay with me."

Two days later, a man in Oklahoma City called and said, "Could you guys use an RV?"

I said, "Yeah. What kind is it?"

This RV is nicer than my own house.

I almost feel embarrassed trying to tell people about my ministry because I don't know how to explain it. I don't have a strategy. All I know is that God most often speaks to us what He will do, we follow, and He does it.

The question is, are we listening enough to hear what He's saying?

I think the world would stand in line to find answers to life's questions. And they're always going to science or the government to get answers because so few people hear the secrets of God that unlock the treasures. Where are the people who are intimate enough with Jesus and who will take time to sit in His presence and listen to His voice?

I was in a church in South Carolina, and I was preaching on the gifts of the Spirit. At the end people were at the altar praying. I looked at this big guy with Afro hair. He was sitting on the front row, but he wasn't praying. The Holy Spirit told me information about him that I could never have guessed.

I said to him, "Who are you? What are you doing here?"

He told me his name and said, "Someone told me to come. He said I would enjoy you."

"Really? Well, I'm going to say something to you. So don't punch me." He nodded. "You're in trouble. Your marriage is in trouble. You did some things you feel really ashamed about, but God wants to heal your marriage. Can I pray for you?"

"How'd you know all that?"

"I don't know anything, dude. Can I pray for that?"

I prayed for him, and the power of God hit him. He fell over in the Spirit and was radically saved. He finally rose up and said, "What was that?"

"I don't know." I just walked away. And that was that.

Later I was doing a conference in Ashland, Kentucky, and that same man was there. When I had first prayed for him, he was separated from his wife. This time he and his wife drove ten hours with their three kids to come to the conference because their marriage got better than it had ever been because God healed their marriage.

All of that happened because the Holy Spirit spoke something to me about that man and his marriage. Then I spoke it to him.

I'm wondering if God wants to speak to all of us.

Jesus is our best friend who will never leave us. He'll never forsake us. He wants to share the secrets in His heart with us so we can unlock the treasures in people's hearts.

I'm to the point in my life where I'm no longer shaped by having an absentee dad while I was growing up, or losing my fortune, or by traveling and living away from everybody I love. I've come to the point where the presence of God's Spirit is what shapes me.

Giving Birth

Jesus says in John 16:14, "He will glorify Me, for He will take of Mine and will disclose it to you."

Think about that. The Holy Spirit will take everything that belongs to Jesus and give it to us. Can you believe it?

Jesus goes on to say, "A little while, and you will no longer see Me; and again a little while, and you will see Me." The disciples wonder what He means, and He explains. "Truly, truly, I say to you, that you will weep and lament, but the world will rejoice; you will grieve, but your grief will be turned into joy" (John 16:16–20).

Jesus is speaking of the fact that the world will rejoice when they see Jesus dead the next afternoon. But Jesus can see that Sunday morning is coming and that His men will be delirious with joy when they see Him again, risen from the dead. Isn't this still true today? Nonbelievers are always looking for ways to discredit Christian beliefs or attack Bible believers. Yet Jesus keeps showing up among us through His Spirit. And we—not they—are the ones who end up rejoicing. I'm happy just talking about it.

Then He says in John 16:21, "Whenever a woman is in labor she has pain, because her hour has come; but when she gives birth to the child, she no longer remembers the anguish because of the joy that a child has been born into the world."

That's weird. Jesus, why are you talking about a woman who's pregnant when you're talking to eleven guys? The first time I read that I wondered, "Who put that in my Bible?" He's talking to eleven men about a woman when she's in labor about to give birth.

In John 13 Jesus teaches us to get low, get slow, get humble, and get broken: Wash feet. "Recognize that I want you to love each other the way I love you." In John 14 it's, "I'm going to the cross so you can be filled with Me and you can do the same things I do, and even greater. I want you to be My Spirit's dwelling place." In chapter 15 it's, "Stay connected to Me. Abide in Me. Live in Me. Become so tight with Me that everything I do, I do through you." In John 16 it's, "Stay intimate with Me. I don't want to just convict you all the time. I want to start sharing My heart with you. I want to share My secrets. I want you to become my 'rhema room.'" Remember, rhema is the Greek word that means "a specific, personal word from the Holy Spirit to your heart."

And then out of nowhere, Jesus says, "Oh, by the way, when a woman's having a baby, she hurts a lot until the baby comes out. But the baby makes her so happy that she forgets the pain."

I asked God, "Why did you put that verse in the last-night teaching?"

He spoke to my heart, "It's the most important verse in the whole last-night's teaching."

"What do you mean?"

"Because every one of you is like that woman. You're all My bride. And every single one of you is pregnant with the kingdom, with My presence, and with revival. But I can't find people who will stay in the labor room until they give birth because they get tired of the pain, and they leave the room."

After Elijah kills those 450 false prophets, he climbs back up Mount Carmel and says to his servant, "Okay, go look for a cloud. It's going to rain." There are no clouds in the sky when he begins to pray for rain. He sends his servant to look for any clouds—six times. Still no cloud. He sends him a seventh time. The servant reports to Elijah that now there's a tiny cloud the size of a man's hand. Elijah has been squatting down with his head between his knees praying and interceding. He was in a "birthing position," if you will, birthing that rainstorm through prolonged prayer.

In John 7:37–38 we read, "Now on the last day, the great day of the feast, Jesus stood and cried out, saying, 'If anyone is thirsty, let him come to Me and drink. He who believes in Me, as the Scripture said, "From his innermost being will flow rivers of living water."'"

Jesus is saying here that if anyone would dare believe in Him, just as the Scripture says—not taking away from it, not adding to it—thrilling things will happen. Out of our "wombs" will flow rivers of life. The womb is what you give birth through. In Galatians 4:19, even Paul says, "I'm in the pains of childbirth."

The church is to be a birthing room.

Sometimes people have to pray for a hundred years before the birth—the move of God—takes place, and very few people are willing to pay the price for the whole gestation period. That's why revival seems to tarry.

I have four girls, two daughters and two daughters-in-law. I love them all. And they've all had babies—fifteen all together. My first daughter, Kristen, is a hard, strong, tough gal, and she's had five kids. When she gives birth, she's amazing. She doesn't let anybody in the room. The door's locked; the lights are out. No TV, no radio. Only her and her husband, and her husband just sits there dying. She just grits it out, and when the baby comes, she cleans it up and he brings it out and shows us. But there's no emotion because she's just determined.

On the other hand, when my daughter April gives birth, it's totally different. She's had three babies. You walk by her door, and she wants you in the room with her. Everybody in the hospital is welcome into her room when she is giving birth. They don't have to be family. She just wants everybody in there with her. So come on in. I'm having a baby. I'm the grandpa, and I don't even want to be in there, but April doesn't care. That's just her.

Tiffany, my older daughter-in-law, is stubborn. She doesn't even want a pain shot, and you do not want to walk into her room because she will say things that you can't believe. She doesn't care because she's in a lot of pain. She's had three. No pain medicine. If I were a woman, I'd want to get a shot the first week I'm pregnant and just stay doped up for nine months. But not Tiffany.

Now my younger daughter-in-law, Hailey, had her first baby. She went through fifty-six hours of labor. Come on, have the kid!

All my girls had their babies differently. Here's my point, you don't have to be like anybody else. God created you to be just as you are, and you need to give birth just as you do. You may not be able to do it like Brooklyn Tabernacle or Christ City, or any other church or Christian. And you may not be able to do it like Cali, Columbia, but maybe you could do the way that's right for people in your town.

But you have to stick with it in the birthing room of prayer and seeking God.

People look at me and say, "How come you don't stand up when we're singing, and how come you don't get on your knees when we're praying?"

You have no idea what I'm doing inside. It's none of your business. It is between Jesus and me. And the same is true for you.

I promise you, you have no idea what I do all day long in prayer, in my birthing position. I'm not going to talk about it because it's nobody's business. I don't see what I see because I'm Dan Bohi. I see what I see because I'm willing to do what God tells me to do because life is in His voice.

Every single one of us is pregnant because God's Word is seed. It's life. A word coming from God created the universe, and a word from God could change it.

A guy named John Wesley was one of nineteen kids. He was like, "Uh, where do I fit in to what God's doing?" He was on a boat going from England to America. And in a massive storm he heard these people worshiping. He said to himself, "I don't have what they have." He didn't hear a sermon. He heard worship coming out the belly of a boat where the poor people traveled. Wesley was on a higher deck because he had more money than they had. He was above them. They were below him. Maybe that's the key. Let's get lower.

Wesley heard this worship coming up from below his deck on that storm-tossed ship. He instantly knew he needed what they had. Right there he had an encounter with God. Now John Wesley is known by everybody, and the people on the boat didn't even preach a sermon. They just gave birth. They gave birth through singing, praise, worship, and faith in God during a terrible storm.

Then John 16:32 Jesus foretells something that will challenge this giving birth. "Behold, an hour is coming, and has already come, for you to be scattered, each to his own home, and to leave Me alone; and yet I am not alone, because the Father is with Me."

The Greek word Jesus uses here for "scattered" is usually not a good word. This is a word that can describe the thinking of liberal theology. It's a word used to describe people who are pulled by their own impulses instead of God's impulse, because until we become the womb of God, until we become the channel of God, until we become the *rhema* room of God, we're left to our own opinions, attitudes, and fears.

We're left to our own thinking, and when it's hard here, then we go the other way. God may want us to go that way, but if we're not being led by His impulse, then we're just "scattered."

"Scatter" can also be used in a good way, as in those who are scattered among the nations. Those are people who are scattered because God spread them out intentionally as "seed." They were the seed in His hands, and He was pleased to throw them out as good seed because they trusted Him with wherever He chose to sow or scatter them. I want to be the good scattered-by-God seed.

My whole desire is simply this: I'm chasing after Him. He's in me, and He keeps compelling me to go. I am His scattered-on-purpose-for-His-purposes gospel seed. His love compels me. His *agape* love is like fuel in my spirit. It moves me, and every other like-minded person, to be that seed that gives birth to the work of God.

When Jesus Prays

Let's look at John 17. This is the high priestly prayer of Jesus Christ.

In *Dressed to Kill* Rick Renner describes six kinds of prayer in the New Testament: consecration, the prayer of faith, supplication, thanksgiving, musing, and intercession. The prayer most used in the whole New Testament—the New Covenant, Matthew to Revelation—is the prayer of consecration.

One hundred thirty-seven verses in the New Testament involve realizing you're in over your head, and you can't pull it off. So you give up everything to God and say, "God, come to our rescue. I surrender it all. I'm Yours. Wherever You take me, I'm all in because I've tried everything, and I can't try anything else. You're the last thing, and now all I want is you." These 137 verses essentially tell us to die. Do you think we're hardheaded?

Just think with me. One hundred and thirty-seven prayers tell us to consecrate ourselves, or get dead enough, so we can be temples for the Holy Spirit without stuff in the way. Jesus wants us dead enough so that we are finally vessels fit for the King. We're like a house fit for the King, where every closet, every crawl space, every attic place, has nothing in it. All the bad stuff is gone. Our whole being is swept clean by the presence of God, and when that's the case, then we don't have to worry about how to pray. He'll pray through us because we'll agree with Him, because we'll go into His presence. Our hearts will never condemn us because our hearts and His heart are the same heart. When we pray this way, we know that He's listening because everything we ask of Him is what He is pleased to do anyway.

Wouldn't it be amazing, if all we would pray are prayers that He is pleased to answer? Guess what prayer that is. It's His prayer. It's His prayer that always gets answered.

I think John 17 is an example of what it looks like for a person to pray from heaven over situations on the earth. Romans 8:26 speaks of the Spirit interceding for us, and John 17 is that prayer modeled for us. Though John 17 is an example of intercessory prayer, it's not merely Jesus' prayer. It's the prayer of the Father's heart through a man named Jesus, who is praying it.

He lifts His eyes to heaven and starts off speaking these words, "Father, the hour has come; glorify Your Son, that the Son may glorify You."

How does God the Father glorify the God the Son? He let's Him die on the cross. So in essence, Jesus is saying, "Let Me die. I want to die in obedience to You, Father. Let Me get to the cross, and then You get glory."

Applied to us, the apostle Paul tells us in Romans 6:11 to reckon, or consider, ourselves dead so Christ can resurrect us.

Now check out these next verses. "Even as You gave Him authority over all flesh, that to all whom You have given Him, He may give eternal life. This is eternal life, that they may know You, the only true God, and Jesus Christ whom You have sent" (John 17:2–3).

We don't think much about this until we read it carefully and think about it. He's not praying from His body here. He's praying from a heavenly realm over Himself because He's praying in third person.

John is the only disciple who received the revelation from the Holy Spirit to write the last night's events in this depth. He wrote it down for us so that we could be privileged to know what God originally shared with only eleven people.

Famous Christian writers like Watchman Nee, Andrew Murray, and E. M. Bounds all believed and taught that we can live in such a way with Jesus to where we are broken enough that our spirit is released, and the Holy Spirit can pray through us from heaven.

Jesus is our example. Part of His pattern for us is how He prayed. And here in John 17 Jesus models true intercession. We allow our flesh, our emotions, our being, to get so broken that our spirit is released from the confines of our flesh. Our spirit is set free and prays from the heavenly perspective over our situation in the earthly realm.

Jesus didn't say, "As You gave Me authority," but rather, "as You gave Him authority over all flesh, that to all whom You have given Him, He may give eternal life."

His spirit is right with his Dad. He is praying from heaven's promises over Himself. He's so broken. His Spirit is free to pray from the unlimited possibilities over Himself.

Then He comes back into His own identity and prays in the first person.

John 17:4 is the keynote verse of this whole prayer: "I glorified You on the earth, having accomplished the work which You have given Me to do." Followed by verse 5, "Now, Father, glorify Me together with Yourself, with the glory which I had with You before the world was."

So He says, "Father, I've glorified You on the earth. I finished the work You sent Me to do." Think about this. He hasn't yet been arrested. Nobody has yet spit on Him. No thorns, no nails, no lashes— yet. He just finishes praying from heaven over Himself and essentially says, "I did it, Dad. Now glorify Me with You." Similarly, as we glorify God, He reflects His glory back down on us as we humbly serve Him.

There have been times when I've allowed myself to get broken to the point where He prayed through me. And every single time I let that happen, my prayers got answered. I don't live there. I don't know about you, but I don't live in a continual state of that kind of intercession.

But I do want to connect with heaven when I pray. So I say, "Lord, I want a deeper revelation of who You are. I believe You can do through me what You did while You were doing it through Yourself here on earth, because the same Spirit that was in You is in me. So, Lord, I should be doing the same things You did, and even greater. Because You, Jesus, said, 'Truly, truly, I say to you, he who believes in Me, the works that I do, he will do also; and greater works than these he will do; because I go to the Father'" (John 14:12).

I don't know how to pray. I just spend about eight hours a day in the Word, listening to God. And after that I try to go out and heal the sick and raise the dead and cast out demons and cleanse lepers as Jesus told us to.

I don't try to go out and be a better pray-er. I try to go out and do what He tells me to do by spending time in Him and giving birth to the kingdom so I don't have to strive uphill. I'm just flowing down stream with the Spirit.

Some might say, "Why don't you pray?"

I pray all the time so I can learn how to pray. I'll wake up in the middle of the night and pray. All day long I can't stop praying. I don't even know if I'm praying right, except I know I can't stop talking to Him because I need to hear from Him. Last night's words from Jesus are not good enough for tonight.

I can get disappointed because I want to see more miracles, but I'm not disappointed with God. It's not on His end, I'm disappointed with me.

I don't want to pray for a woman and she gets healed and then pray for a man and he dies. I'd like to get the words Jesus tells me clearly in my heart so that I can pray as He wants me to pray.

I don't pray asking God for a lot of things. I pray asking God, "Please change me into more of You so You can start doing what You want to do through me. God, would You please take all these roadblocks out of my mind?"

I am so tired of the lies that are in my life. I am so tired of believing that God can heal this depression, but that terminal disease for which there's no cure, well, that's harder for God to heal.

Where do these lies come from? Not from Jesus. My whole prayer life seems like, "God, would you please change me so I can be like You, my Father?"

When We Listen to the Spirit

When my son, Chad, was backslidden, I was at a prayer meeting, and all these college kids had their hands on me and were praying. I was telling the Lord that I didn't know how to pray for my boy.

The Holy Spirit said, "Good. Now I can pray."

Then the Spirit said to me, "I want you to go home now. I've got your boy. Don't worry about it. I've got him."

So I went home. The next night we were at prayer meeting. My son walked into that prayer meeting. Nobody invited him, but he was under conviction, and I was happy.

Do you ever get happy when you've been praying for somebody

who's so hard headed and then they come under conviction? You know they can't win because God's bigger.

My son stumbled into that prayer meeting. He was on the second row and he knelt down. I snuck up behind him and heard him pray, "God, I don't ever deserve to feel You because I've abused Your grace. You've given me so much. And I took advantage of it. But if You could make me holy, if You could just make me holy, I will live for You the rest of my life."

When did that happen? It happened about seventeen hours after the Holy Spirit told me, "Go home, I've got him. You don't have to worry anymore." You know why it happened? It happened because the Holy Spirit's prayers always get answered.

Another time I was preaching at College Church in Olathe, Kansas, and Pastor Sam Vassal was there during the revival, and the Holy Spirit said to me, "I want you to take him out and pray with him."

I said, "Why?"

"Don't worry about it. Just go pray with him."

So I took him in my red truck and we drove to a little lake. I asked him, "Can I pray for you?"

"Sure thing."

He didn't know me. I didn't know him. But I put my hand on his shoulder, and I got in the Spirit and lost track of time as the Spirit prayed through me.

After a while the Spirit said, "Okay, you're done. Take him back to his hotel."

I said, "I'm done." And I took him back to his hotel. The next week he called and said, "Brother Dan, when you prayed for me, my heart was only at 13 percent capacity of what it should be. And when I got back, I went to the doctor, and my heart was at 68 percent." And he asked me, "When can you do a revival for me?"

"Whoa, what do you mean?"

"I was on the transplant list. But when you prayed for me, God healed my heart."

How did that happen? It happened because *the Holy Spirit's prayers always get answered.*

The Lord first called me to this full-time ministry in 2009. I was so excited. I was praying and getting ready. I had two meetings in Southern California. I was so pumped because I had two meetings.

Then the Holy Spirit said, "I want you to pack for a month."

"Why? I only have meetings for ten days."

"Just pack for a month."

That morning at church in Gardner, Kansas, the pastor asked me to pray because he understood that I had a grace on me for healing.

I said, "Okay."

I was going down the line, laying hands on people, and praying for them. I came to a lady, and all of a sudden I got into the Spirit. I lost track of time as I was praying. I don't even know what I was praying because I felt absorbed into Him. This kind of thing can happen when we get past ourselves and let the Holy Spirit use us as his prayer room.

So as I was praying for this lady, I finally said, "Thank You, Lord."

Instantly, the pain left her, and I felt it leave her body and shoot through my hand. My hand was hot for an hour. I didn't know what had happened, so I called Gordon Wetmore, the president of Nazarene Theological Seminary at that time. He was on my board. He's smart.

I told him about my hand heating up. "What was that, Gordon?"

"That's the anointing of God."

"Oh."

The next day I packed up and drove to El Centro, California, to start the revival meeting. A pastor came up and said, "Would you pray for me? I have a heart problem, and in the morning I'm supposed to have three stents put in."

I said, "Sure." But my hand wasn't hot anymore. I thought it still might have some "Holy Spirit residue" on it. But it wasn't hot. So maybe I didn't have any more of that anointing.

I put my hand on him anyway and said, "Lord, heal his heart."

And the next night he came back, and I asked, "How's your heart?"

"They didn't have to put the stents in."

"What do you mean?"

"They went in, prepared to do the angioplasty, but they didn't have to do it. They put the dye in and everything had already opened up. There's no cholesterol. I used to have 380 bad cholesterol, but now there's no plaque."

That pastor called his district superintendent. That district superintendent called me and said, "Can you go to this other church?" That district superintendent called another district superintendent. That second superintendent said, "I have three churches where you could come." I spent five weeks in California instead of the ten days I thought I had lined up. The Holy Spirit knows what will happen before we do.

When I tell you this, it's not for me, a preacher who travels around in a car. It's for the body of Christ, the church. It's for the royal priesthood. I'm wondering if we're willing to live intimately enough with Jesus for the Holy Spirit to be able to pray through us. Are we?

I want to walk into a hospital room and let Jesus reach through my hands and touch and heal the one who is sick. I'm really trying to get lower before the Lord so He can flow through me.

I'm not telling you these things so you will look at me. I'm telling you these things so when you look at me, you'll say, "There's no way you could do that. That must be God."

That's exactly what I'm trying to point out. I myself can't do anything. I'm trying to get low enough and little enough and out of the way enough so Jesus can do everything in me and through me. I'm not there yet. But I'm running that way.

I used to think the bigger venues and the bigger crowds were where it was all at. I don't think that way anymore. I think it's just wherever God draws desperate people. That's where I want to be. I don't care if it's fifteen people or five. I just want to be where He's at and where He is working.

Hearing the Logos and Rhema

In John 17:6–8 Jesus uses two Greek words for "word" in two very different ways. One is the revealed Word (*logos*) as Jesus' incarnation, as the objective message, and as it's written down as Scripture. The other is the immediate, personal word (*rhema*) spoken to us for a particular purpose.

> *"I have manifested Your name to the men whom You gave Me out of the world; they were Yours and You gave them to Me, and they have kept Your word [logos]. Now they have come to know that everything You have given Me is from You; for the words [rhemata] which You gave Me I have given to them; and they received them and truly understood that I came forth from You, and they believed that You sent Me."*

In one sentence He says they have kept, or guarded, God's *logos*, the revealed Word, the spoken Word that's recorded. In the next sentence He says He gave them *rhema*, the personal, revealed word from heaven.

In Matthew 4:4 Jesus uses this same term when He says that we are to live on "every word [*rhema*] that proceeds out of the mouth of God." This expectation of His confirms that God still speaks to us this way today.

We know the Father's heart through Jesus. If we're dead to self and filled with Jesus' life, then we don't have to worry about how we're doing or how well we're speaking. We just have to speak what the Word of God tells us to speak—that is, His *rhema*, His revealed, spoken Word from heaven to our listening, waiting heart.

And if we're willing to listen and be obedient to speak what God tells us to speak, then maybe somebody in the room may get delivered. Somebody may get born again. Somebody may get baptized in the Holy Spirit. Somebody may get healed of cancer.

Our responsibility for this is to stay full of God's presence and release what He tells us to release. He does the work.

The best example of that happening is when Jesus says the exact same words to the other ten guys that night, and John's the only one who gets enough *rhema* to write down what's now called the Upper Room Discourse.

Jesus has a lot of things to tell all of us, but a lot of us can't handle it. So He only reveals things to us at the level we're willing to receive them. Everything He reveals to us that we're not willing to receive will heap condemnation on us because we're held accountable for the light that we have. I want to get to the place where Jesus doesn't have to hold anything back that He wants to share with me.

In John 17:11 Jesus prays, "I am no longer in the world; and yet they themselves are in the world, and I come to You. Holy Father, keep them in Your name, the name which You have given Me, that they may be one even as We are."

The whole thing is about intimacy. The whole night in the upper room Jesus is teaching us to become one with God.

John 17:15 says, "I do not ask You to take them out of the world, but to keep them from the evil one."

Notice the phrase "evil one." The word "one" is not in the original Greek. It is a word added by translators and editors to help us understand the text better—they think. But sometimes the words in italics found in the Bible do *not* help us. Sometimes they inadvertently mislead us.

There are different views on this, but I am convinced that in this verse the added word "one" is misleading. It makes us focus on Satan, the Evil One. But it's a bad addition. If you look at any original manuscript, the word "one" is not in there.

So what is Jesus really saying here? Is He talking about Satan? No. What He's saying is, Father, keep them from "the *ponerou* [evil]."

Jesus is talking about the wicked, evil nature of sin that every single one of us were born with. And what he's praying is, "Father, please keep them safe from themselves until they realize who I want to turn them into."

The devil is not your problem. He's already under your feet. He's just ticked off because he lost. He's not your problem. I'm so tired of hearing people talk about the devil. If you're that aware of the devil, where's God in your life?

I'm to the point I'm not worried about sin. I'm not worried about the devil. I'm just worried about my own stinking thinking.

The main thing keeping me from realizing that I'm the gate of heaven is my brain that keeps getting in the way. I have to unlearn things I learned earlier in my Christian life. I'm trying to be re-educated.

Acts 4:13 tells us that the disciples were ordinary and uneducated. But they had spent a lot of time with Jesus. They came across a man who hadn't walked for forty years. But there is power in the name of Jesus, and they healed him by that power.

Where did they learn that? They learned that by hanging out with Jesus. How do you get people healed who have been lame from their mother's womb? Just hang out with Jesus long enough, believe in Him and His power, and use His name—the representation of who He is— with faith.

Jesus is praying, "God, keep them from the nature of evil that's in them because My sacrifice will be able to solve the problem they were born with."

Then Jesus prays, "Sanctify them in the truth; Your word is truth" (verse 17).

He is praying: "Father, make them holy. Make them morally undefiled. Make them clean. Make them pure, sanctified by the truth. Your word is truth." And then He declares that He's sending them into the world.

In John 17:21 He prays "that they may all be one; even as You, Father, are in Me and I in You, that they also may be in Us, so that the world may believe that You sent Me."

Jesus knows that the only way His men could ever be willing to be one as the Trinity is one is if they truly let Him sanctify them through and through so that everything in their spirit, soul, and body that's ashamed and embarrassed and afraid to really believe is gone. Jesus knows He is able to do this. He knows His followers can be cleansed, purified, sanctified; and everything that holds them back can be removed.

Prophecies and a Cleansed Heart

The prophet who got the most *rhema* about Jesus was Isaiah, hundreds of years before Jesus was born. In Isaiah 6 the prophet sees how gloriously holy God is. He's undone because there are things in him that are "unclean." God sends fire from the altar in heaven, and the fire touches and cleanses Isaiah's lips.

God then says, "Now your sin is atoned for." He didn't say, "your sins." He means, "The nature of sin that you're born with—it's purged out of you. It's cleansed away." Then Isaiah no longer says, "Woe is me."

Now that his sin nature has been cleansed, Isaiah says, "I'll go for you, Lord. I'm ready now because there's nothing in me that's not like You." He was truly transformed and purified.

If that could happen to Isaiah, I wonder if it could happen to us.

Jeremiah 31:33 promises that God will take what's written in our Bibles, and write it on our hearts to be His living epistles. We will stop speaking our opinions and our hot air, and we will start letting His Word come out of us.

In Psalm 51 we see David saying, "Lord, I'm a sinner. I've been a sinner since I was in my mama's belly. I was a sinner knit together in her womb. Please forgive my sin, but don't stop there. Cleanse me. Give me a pure heart. Give me a sustaining spirit."

"The problem with me, God, goes beyond the fact that beautiful bathing Bathsheba was so good looking. My deeper problem is that my heart still has things in it that aren't like You. Would you please give me a pure heart?"

The problem isn't necessarily in the temptation. The problem is our lack of the power and presence of God. If there's something in you that hasn't let Him take over—give it all over to Him.

Ezekiel says the same thing in chapters 11, 18, and 36. If you'll let Him take your hardened heart out and put His heart in you, then it makes room for you to believe that His Spirit could actually fill you and change you radically. When God does this in you, all of your desires become one with His desires. You start doing what He wants you to do, and you start praying what He wants you to pray.

Then in Malachi 3 the Lord says, "I'm like a launderer's soap. You have sin stains, but I have the problem solved. I'll take it out of the fiber of who you are. But if you'll let Me, I won't stop there. I'll put you on the Bunsen burner, and I'll heat you up with My fire. I'll take the dross away, and you'll be such a reflection of Me."

This happened to me at 5:37 p.m., June 15, 1995. I tried my whole life to be holy. You can't try enough to be holy.

I finally said, "Okay, I give up. Yes, I'm yours." And out of nowhere the Holy Spirit did it in me. I had no idea the Holy Spirit could do that. But He changed all my desires instantly. I no longer cared only about me. I now cared about others.

I was lying in a hospital, and I no longer cared about my comfort. I cared about the nurses, and I actually started believing that I could do the things the Bible said because it was no longer simply a theory or a theology—it became genuine reality.

Be Sanctified

Six hundred and eleven verses in the Bible say you need to be sanctified. Twenty-five verses in the Bible say you need to be born again. You need to be justified. You need to be regenerated. You need to be adopted. Twenty-five verses say you need to get in the family of God, and 611 verses say, after you're in the family, you need to let God make you pure and holy as He is holy. Think about that. Twenty-five verses compared to 611 verses. I wonder which one the Lord is more concerned about.

I didn't know He could make me holy. You don't have to know that He can do it. You just have to want Him to do it. He could give you a pure heart today. He can take everything out of you that's not like Him. You could actually start believing that He can do through you everything the Spirit did through Jesus.

The disciples of Jesus had been with Jesus for three years. Yet every single one of them still needed to be sanctified.

How about you? Do you need the Spirit of God to sanctify you?

When you're a believer, your head might get mad at a message like this. But your heart's drawn to it. And a battle may be going on in the fourteen inches between your head and your heart.

I'm so tired of people running up to the altar and never changing because they run up to the front of the church out of impulses that are from their emotions. They don't come from their spirit. A lot of people have been to the altar a hundred times, and they still don't live in the reality of the kingdom.

Romans 12 calls us to lay our lives down as living and holy sacrifices. I want to be cleansed, holy, and live like Jesus. I don't want there to be anything in me that isn't in Him. I want Him to take all my selfish sin away and sanctify me.

When I got sanctified, I've never recovered because it was real. If He could do that for me, you might be a cakewalk for Him.

So right now I want you to ask your best friend, the Holy Spirit, "Lord, search my heart. Look at my heart. Test me. Try me. Peel back my layers of defense." Ask Him to get real with you.

This means if the Holy Spirit has said to you, "Right now is your moment, I want to sanctify you and make you like My Son." He wants to sanctify you right now.

Is the Holy Spirit telling you right now that you don't have this experience? Is the Spirit telling you that's why you don't live in His life? Is this why you live in depression? Fear? Is this why you live bitter and hurt? Is it because you're not all in, and you're still holding onto something?

If there's nothing in you but Him, it's hard to get hurt. Right now you can say, "God, I want a pure heart. I want to be sanctified."

God's called you. Give yourself to Him as a living sacrifice. Do it right now where you are.

It will change you forever.

PART 5

Doing the Word Then and Now

As we've seen through John 13–17, Jesus teaches that we can really live love as He did. He teaches that we can be servants and go low the way He did. We can actually be the dwelling place where the Spirit lives, and we can do what He did—and even greater things. He also teaches that we can flow in the power of the Spirit because we live in intimacy with Him, we abide in Him, and we don't have to try to do it on our own. He encourages us to stay weak enough and dependent enough on Him to continually cling to Him. And because of our abiding in Him, He'll share His deepest secrets with us, and we'll become the intercessors that God intends to pray and work through.

Did His disciples actually do what He prophesied over them? Yes, they did.

Jesus, Peter, and Paul

We can find amazing similarities between the life and ministry of Jesus and the life and ministries of His men. Let's look at a few. Luke, a doctor, wrote the books of Luke and Acts. And he teaches us more about the Holy Spirit than any other Bible author.

Luke writes extensively about the miracle working activity of Jesus, Peter, and Paul. He demonstrates that Jesus' men follow in His footsteps and operate in the same power of the Holy Spirit that their Master lived in and demonstrated.

Dr. Luke wants us to recognize that Jesus' men share parallel ministries with their Lord. Like Jesus, His men were also prophets, healers, preachers, and exorcists. Now He intends us to do the same ministries that He did (John 14:12). By His power and anointing, we will become prophets, healers, preachers, and exorcists.

Notice the similarities of Jesus' ministry, Peter's ministry, and Paul's ministry. If you didn't know who they were, you could hardly tell them apart.

First, we see God's wrath. In Luke, Jesus clears the money changers out of the temple because His wrath is against idolatry and abuse of God's house of worship. In Acts 5 Peter prophesizes the death of Ananias and Sapphira as he expresses the wrath of God against deceitfulness in the house of worship. Then in Acts 13 Paul encounters a sorcerer named Elymas, who's trying to turn the proconsul away from faith in Christ. Paul blinds him as he expresses God's wrath against deceitfulness and fraud. Jesus, Peter, and Paul all display the wrath of God against things that are deceitful in the realm of faith.

I'm kind of glad I haven't had this kind of ministry experience yet.

Second, we see faith for healing. In Luke 5 four guys cut a hole in the roof to lower their paralyzed friend so Jesus can heal him. Jesus sees their faith, says to the paralyzed guy, "Your sins are forgiven," and the man is healed. In Acts 3:1–10 Peter and John see a lame man who's been begging his whole life. Peter fixes his eyes on him, and he must have seen faith because he heals the guy. Then in Acts 14:8–18 Paul meets a lame guy, fixes his eyes on him and sees that he has faith to be healed, and heals him. Jesus sees faith in people. So does Peter. So does Paul.

This kind of thing still happens. One day I was at a church in Texas. During the worship time the Holy Spirit said, "Turn around. I want to show you something." I was sitting on the front row as I always do. I turned around and saw a guy bending over on a cane. I kept looking at him because I felt that the Spirit was telling me to look at him. I stared at him, right in the eyes, and I could see he had faith to be healed.

Then I prayed, "God, he has faith to be healed, just heal him right now."

And the man threw down his cane.

He walked right up in front of the whole church of about 400 people and said, "I fell off a telephone pole thirty years ago. My back was broken in five places. I've been in pain for thirty years. And when you were staring at me, all the pain left."

Third, we see freedom from bondage. In Luke 8 Jesus meets a raging demoniac, and he casts the legion of demons out of him to set the man free. And in Luke 9 Jesus gives authority to all the disciples to cast out demons. In Acts 16 Paul and Silas cast a money-making-future-predicting demon out of a slave girl; her owner gets so mad he has Paul and Silas thrown in prison. Then when they worship God, their chains fall off—and all the other prisoners' as well.

This kind of thing also happens today in all kinds of ways, especially in spiritual deliverance.

Fourth, we see individual healings. In Luke 4 Jesus heals Peter's mother-in-law, who'd had a bad fever. In John 5 Jesus heals one man at the pool of Bethesda. Why just one? I don't know. In Acts 9 Peter heals Aeneas who had been paralyzed for eight years. In Acts 19:11 God heals many individuals through Paul, even through contact with handkerchiefs and aprons.

Praise God that we see many individuals get healed.

Fifth, we see cases where everyone gets healed. In Luke 6:19 power is going out of Jesus, and he heals all the people who come to Him. In Acts 5:15–16 Peter is so full of God's power that everyone who comes to him is healed, even those who only get under his shadow. In Acts 19 Paul's ministry in Ephesus over a two-year period finds extraordinary healing miracles happening that impact the whole populace. Then when Paul is shipwrecked on the island of Malta in Acts 28, everybody on the island who is sick gets healed through him.

I want to see gatherings where everyone gets healed.

Sixth, we see raising people from the dead. In Luke 8 Jairus' sick daughter dies because Jesus is a little late getting there, and He raises her from the dead. In Acts 9 Tabitha has died, and when Peter is summoned, he sends all the mourners out of the room, prays, then raises her from the dead. In Acts 20 Paul preaches a long sermon, and a guy named Eutychus who's sitting in a window dozes off, falls three stories, and dies. Paul goes down and lays on him and raises him from the dead.

This happens on occasion, and I hope to see more.

Looking at these six areas of manifesting God's power, we can hardly tell the ministries of Jesus, Peter, and Paul apart. How did that happen? They had the fulfillment of what Jesus taught about in the Upper Room Discourse of John 13–17.

And it all began to happen in Acts 2.

We cannot say that a miracle happened just because it was Jesus—or that He set us up for failure because we haven't experienced these miracles in our own lives. He did not give the Spirit so that He could be powerful for the first thirty years of Christianity and then leave us on our own. The promises and expectations of John 13–17 are for us too.

Authority—Ours or God's?

For a long time I had a problem with joint pain. It was hard to stand up because my hips and my ankles and my knees and my feet hurt. And now I've been being accused of preaching more than two hours—while standing up—because I don't have pain in my joints anymore.

When I started walking, it hurt so bad, but I just believed that the power of Jesus and His name was enough to heal all my joints. I believed that, and I didn't want to get arthritis or lubrication medicine.

I didn't want to go to the doctor because I thought, "When will I ever believe His name is enough? When will I ever deeply listen to His voice? When will I ever believe there's truly power in His name?"

I'm not against doctors. I'm thankful for doctors. But when am I going to believe the way they did in the book of Acts?

On every step of my walks I prayed, "Thank you, God, that You heal my joints." I wasn't trying to memorize some mantra to earn His approval. I thanked him by faith for my healing—before I was healed. It came from the depths of my heart. "Thank you, God, that my feet won't hurt anymore. Thank you, God, that my knees don't hurt. Thank you that Your healing is mine. Thank you, Lord, that my back doesn't hurt. And my hips don't hurt. Thank you, Jesus, that my pelvis doesn't hurt."

I don't even know when it all happened. But it did. Every joint gradually stopped hurting. Jesus healed me.

The more we read this Bible and actually believe it, the more we will change the world around us to never be the same.

Aren't you glad that God's power has not diminished? Aren't you glad that we're not on this earth merely for our own interests? Aren't you glad He didn't put us here so the best we could do is have a "nice day?" Aren't you glad that rather He put us on the earth so He could show His power and love to the world through us?

Let's remind ourselves of the background. In Acts 1 Jesus says, "Go to Jerusalem and don't leave until you get the promise of the Father—the Holy Spirit's coming. Because when He comes, you'll get power. You'll be witnesses. You won't be able to keep quiet. Now go to Jerusalem and wait."

So the disciples go to Jerusalem, and Acts 1:14 says, "These all with one mind were continually devoting themselves to prayer, along with the women, and Mary the mother of Jesus, and with His brothers."

They all continue with prayer in one accord, or "one mind"—earnestly, continually, and humbly they keep pursuing this promise of God that He will pour out the Holy Spirit on them.

It's probably just the disciples at first. And the more they seek God, others start coming until it grows to 120—ten times larger than when they started. We don't know how many days they pray, but at one point Peter stands up and quotes a couple of Psalms and concludes that they have to replace Judas.

He doesn't hear this from God. He's making his own conclusion based on what a couple of Bible verses mean to him. He's not trying to be bad. He's just thinking his own way, not God's. Like Peter, you and I may have what we think is a good idea. There's a lot of that in the church. The question is this: Is it of the Lord? Instead of asking God to bless our ideas, what if we all waited until we were led and empowered by the Holy Spirit, and we said and did only what He wanted us to say and do? I wonder if the results would be better than, "I think we have to do this."

So they draw straws to decide who the twelfth apostle will be. What a way to determine God's will. Actually, it's a joke. And this was the last time in the Bible they ever did it. Matthias is chosen to replace Judas, but we don't see anything about him after this. Clearly, their intent didn't work out. God wasn't in it. But Peter did it because he thought he needed to fill the position. How common is that in the church?

Waiting in Faith

What is God's intent? Jesus' resurrection is very likely on the Jewish Feast of Firstfruits. Jesus walks the earth and appears to people for forty days after His resurrection until He ascends to heaven (Acts 1:3, 9). Then in Acts 2:1 comes the day of Pentecost, also known as the Feast of Weeks. And it comes fifty days after the Feast of Firstfruits. Do the math, and there are ten days between Jesus' ascension and the day of Pentecost. And this time God really gives them something to celebrate.

They're all in one room, they all have the same mind, and they've basically been there for ten days.

With school and ballgames and events and all the activities we think we need to do, how can we ever come together in one accord and wait on God the way the 120 did? We foolishly think that we can do it in a short meeting because we're more sophisticated, and busier, than they were. Remember, these guys spent three years with Jesus before this. Now they've spent the better part of ten days praying and getting into one-accord unity.

We always want to have the same results that the original disciples of Jesus had—but without doing the same things they did.

Then "suddenly," out of nowhere, comes a sound that fills the whole house where they are. Must be a big house for all those people. It sounds like "a violent rushing wind." Think of an intense storm or a hurricane. They weren't expecting it. They didn't know what to expect.

Maybe that's the key. We think revival should be a certain way. We think revival means that everybody gets saved and sanctified and healed and delivered because that's the paradigm we've set up for revival.

The disciples of Jesus didn't know what to expect. Jesus has simply told them to wait until it comes. Well, what's it going to come like? Don't worry about that. Just wait until it comes. Maybe if we stopped putting stipulations on things, He would actually come. He might come in like a storm, but He might come in like a quiet lamb.

This roaring sound of wind from heaven comes and fills the whole house where they're sitting. Now get this: They aren't anguishing. They're past the place where they would run away or lay prostrate in fear because they've gotten to a place where they're all in. They're fully consecrated, and there's nothing left to do. So they sit and rest in faith.

Faith is not quoting every one of the eighty-three healing verses so you can be healed. Faith is not saying the name "Jesus" just right when you pray. It's not saying "in the name of Jesus," with the right accent at the right place.

Faith is a privileged position you're in. It is when you are in the Spirit of God to receive all that He's already purchased. The disciples in Acts 2 finally get to the position where they can receive in faith sitting—not anguishing, not worrying, not pressing. Maybe that's why it took ten days.

Faith is the privileged position that God lets us be in when we live by the Spirit, not by the flesh. What makes it a privileged position is that we're in a position with God where we can receive all that He intends to give because He gives good and perfect gifts.

Too often we ask, "How long will it take?" Who cares? The wait is worth it.

Tongues of Fire

Acts 2:3 tells us, "There appeared to them tongues as of fire." That's the best description they could come up with for what was happening.

These "tongues as of fire" rest on each one of them. That's weird. Why weren't they fiery hearts? Were they big tongues like Mick Jagger's? I'm not being sacrilegious. It's just the way my mind works. Why would He choose tongues? Perhaps it's because He wants us to start speaking the way He speaks. He wants us to speak like Him, because life is in His voice. And if we actually speak His words, we'd probably have more life.

I wonder how long it would take for the world to change if we had these tongues of fire—His tongue of fire. We falsely think we don't need to spend ten days getting the real fire of God on us so we can start talking like God. Instead we get put off and say, "I can't believe that guy did this to me." Then instead of taking it to God and getting a fresh baptism of fire, we call somebody and complain.

Acts 2:4 continues, "They were all filled with the Holy Spirit and they begin to speak with other tongues, as the Spirit was giving them utterance."

Picture this room full of people all speaking these different languages that they had never learned right in the midst of what sounds like a storm.

Someone was speaking Cretan. Someone else was speaking Arabic. Another person was speaking Greek. All these different languages. They're worshiping God, and all of a sudden everything changes.

Acts 2:5–6 says, "Now there were Jews living in Jerusalem, devout men from every nation under heaven. And when this sound occurred, the crowd came together, and were bewildered because each one of them was hearing them speak in his own language."

In Acts 2:6 the Holy Spirit directs Dr. Luke to use a different Greek word for "sound." It's the word *phon-es*. Every other time in the New Testament this word is used, it means "voice." The people outside the upper room heard a "voice."

This is what happened in that room. They spent ten days getting rid of everything that was in the way of them and God, and then He pours out heaven on them. It sounds like a storm to them. The Bible often describes God as lightning and thunder. And inside the room they hear this roaring sound. Now the people outside the room aren't seeking God like the folks inside the room. The people outside the room hear a sound like a "voice."

It's the same sound, except God makes it palatable for wherever you're at on your spiritual journey. The people in the room hear a storm. The people outside hear the voice in their own language.

I wonder how God can do that. It's the same way He could enable you to speak grace instead of retribution. It's the same way God could enable you to speak mercy because you don't have any more rights because now you're becoming love because you gave up your life. There has to come a time when we can't be offended. If not, the gospels are meaningless.

Acts 2:6–8 describes the phenomenon. "And when this sound occurred, the crowd came together, and were bewildered because each one of them was hearing them speak in his own language. They were amazed and astonished, saying, 'Why, are not all these who are speaking Galileans? And how is it that we each hear them in our own language to which we were born?'"

How is this possible? And how in the world could they speak where the listeners couldn't resist it? Maybe it was because they got tongues of fire, His fire.

They have been waiting for ten days. Now they're so saturated and filled with Jesus that when they release the overflow of their heart, it draws everybody in, and they're all amazed. And they want to know, "What does this mean?" (2:12).

Others mockingly say, "Oh, they're just full of sweet wine" (2:13). The word used here for wine is *gleukos*, which means new wine or sweet wine, and it's the word from which we get the English word glucose.

Everybody is totally amazed at what they're hearing and seeing. But some start mocking. No matter what God does, someone will always criticize it or make fun of it.

All the people from these eighteen nations are looking at the 120 from the upper room carrying on, and they're wondering if they're all on a sugar high—or drunk. They're excited and wild.

You know why the world doesn't get saved? It's partly because when most people look into a church, they don't see "*gleukos*-high" people. They see sedation and boredom.

Wouldn't it be great to have an indictment like the folks from the upper room had? "Hey, are you guys high on something?"

God's Rhema

In Acts 2:14 Peter starts preaching on Pentecost. "Peter, taking his stand with the eleven, raised his voice and declared to them: 'Men of Judea and all you who live in Jerusalem, let this be known to you and give heed to my words.'"

Peter *declared*. This word "declared," or "addressed," is a particular word the New Testament uses in connection with an inspired utterance. It indicates that now Peter is speaking out of the impulse of the Holy Spirit.

In Acts 1 Peter said what he did because he thought it was the right thing to say. It's how he had been trained. Too many preachers create and preach a lot of great sermons that come straight out of the Bible—but without waiting until they have been baptized with the Holy Spirit. When that happens, their agenda is woven in with His agenda.

After Acts 2 Peter doesn't have an agenda. The Spirit of God hits him, and he's never the same. Now he speaks out of the empowerment and the utterance that only the Holy Spirit can give him. And when he starts preaching on the day of Pentecost, it isn't just his words, it's the Spirit's words.

That's a big difference, isn't it? Can't you tell when someone is speaking to you from God's heart as opposed to just speaking to you from their own heart? Can't you tell the difference?

When someone speaks to you, and their hearts are deep into the heart of God, then you can tell that their speaking is Christ's agenda and not simply their own. They don't vacillate between the two. It gets so singular.

When Peter says, "Give heed to my words," do you know what term he chooses for "words"? It's *rhema*. He is speaking of the influence of God. And that's *rhema*.

Under this Holy Spirit inspiration, he starts out with humor. "These men are not drunk, as you suppose, for it is only the third hour of the day." The Jewish third hour is 9 a.m. So what's he saying? We don't get drunk until 10 a.m.?

I wish we would laugh more. I think when we get to heaven, we'll see Jesus and He's going to say, "Why were you so serious?" Don't you agree? Think about it.

He'll say, "Look at Satan." We'll look, and Satan will be this bound, defeated loser. Then we'll say, as is prophesied in Isaiah 14:16, "That's him? He's the guy who made the earth tremble?"

In Acts 2 they've prayed so much, they've run out of things to pray. They're just sitting there waiting. Now that they're filled with the Holy Spirit, they can just listen to the Spirit and then say what

God's saying. Because now they are so clean, there's nothing in them that'll get in the way, and He can just speak *rhema* words to them.

The beauty of God's Word is this. Everything written in the Bible is now *logos* words. It was once *rhema* words, and now it is *logos* words. But everything in the Bible, which is *logos*, can in turn become *rhema* words to your soul when the Holy Spirit applies and speaks them personally into your heart.

Every word in the pages of the Bible, every single word, is *logos*. It's heavenly language put on paper. If you want to know Jesus enough, and you are willing to spend time deeply listening to His voice, every single word could become a *rhema* word to you. It could become alive for you.

Every single word.

He could take any verse in the Bible and lead you personally, privately, and intimately with that verse. It could leave the realm of something that *could* happen and become the thing that *is* happening, depending on how much you want to get close to the heart of Jesus.

The Spirit and Jesus

After his opening humor, Peter quotes the prophet Joel. "'And it shall be in the last days,' God says, 'That I will pour forth of My Spirit on all mankind; and your sons and your daughters shall prophesy, and your young men shall see visions, and your old men shall dream dreams'" (Acts 2:16–17).

The first thing Peter preaches out of the upper room, coming from those tongues of fire, is that this manifestation is not just for the 120; this is for everybody who's alive on planet earth. And when it happens, you'll all prophesy. You'll all be able to hear personally from God and speak His words. You'll all speak words that don't originate in you. They originate in God. Isn't that good news?

He says, "Your young men will see visions, and your old men will dream dreams." I can't tell the difference, except one is when you're awake, and the other one is when you're sleeping. When young men are awake and get visions, the visions may not scare them. Because when you're younger, you think you can do anything—until you learn you can't. And God lets old people like me have dreams because in my dreams I have more courage than I would if I were awake. I wake up and say, "What was that?" My dad is in his late 80s, and he dreams all the time. Then he wakes up and says, "I need a pill." Aren't you glad God gives us both visions and dreams?

And aren't you glad that the Lord prompts Peter to say that the Holy Spirit will be poured out on both on men and women? God's not a chauvinist. Both men and women will hear His voice and speak His *rhema* words to the world (Acts 2:17–18).

Peter quotes Joel about freaky signs and wonders in both the heavens and the earth, and then that "everyone who calls on the name of the Lord will be saved" (Acts 2:19–21). The word for "saved" in the Greek is the word *sozo*. Whoever calls on the name of the Lord shall be *sozo* (saved). *Sozo* has a big, wide meaning and can include being forgiven, healed, delivered, set free, made whole, or kept safe and sound.

Some will ask, "Well, how hard do you have to call?"

I don't know. It just says "calls."

Peter goes on to say that Jesus was crucified by godless men, yet by God's foreknowledge and plan, and then He was resurrected because it's impossible for death to hold Him (2:22–23). Death can't hold you either because God's Spirit lives in you. Heaven and earth will pass away, but His Word will never pass away, and His Word lives in you.

When Peter talks about what God did through Jesus, the phrase "through him" is important. The word "through" is the Greek word *dia*, from which we get the root word with the same meaning in English. The signs, the wonders, the miracles didn't come from Jesus. They came from the Father through Jesus. He was the channel. He was the catalyst, the dwelling place of the Holy Spirit. He was the *rhema* room.

That's also why Jesus can say in John 14:12 that you and I will do the same things He did, and even greater—because He wants to do those things through us.

Jesus is saying, "I heard what the Father said to say, and I said it. I saw what He said to do, and I did it. It didn't originate with Me; it originated in the heart of the Father. If you've seen Me, you've seen the Father. And I'm imparting to you what the Father gave Me. As the Father sent Me, in the same way I am sending you."

Isn't that good news? You could go into a situation feeling absolutely empty, and that's probably a good position to be in and a good way to feel, because then there's room for Him to do whatever He wants to do through you. But if you have it all planned out and all figured out, you may not leave room for the Spirit's leading.

If you go into a counseling session and you have it all planned out, you'll be thinking, "I'm going to counsel him this way, and I'm going to tell him this truth." On the other hand, if you go into a situation, and you are totally depending on the Lord, you can pray, "God, tell me what to say. I don't know what to say, but I am trusting You to guide me and speak to me so that I only speak your *rhema* words."

David's Affirmation

Peter continues preaching, and in Acts 2:25–28 he quotes King David in affirming that the Christ lives and is present with us. What's David's quote here for?

When I see something like that in my Bible, I usually look past it to the important stuff. Have you ever done that? When you're reading your Bible and you see something in there from the Old Testament, don't just skip over it. Rather ask yourself, "Why is this here?" Ask the Lord, "Why did you put this in here, Lord?"

I asked that about this quote from David. Then one day I was listening to the Holy Spirit as He was trying to teach me who He was: "This first sermon by Peter is a picture of Word and Spirit, of purity and power."

In Acts 2:25 Peter quotes from Psalm 16:8, "I saw the LORD always in my presence." David is saying that he always sees by faith that God is with him. He sees by faith. It's like Hebrews 12:2, looking to Jesus because He perfects my faith. Or 2 Corinthians 3:18, beholding Him and looking to Him in faith.

That's when I start seeing the image of Him and what He's doing in me. I become what I'm looking at because I'm looking at Him in me.

By faith I've realized that God never takes His gaze off me. By faith I've realized He never loses track of who He knows I am—even in the times I was in sin. When you realize how much He really loves you, and you don't forget that, isn't it a lot easier to trust Him no matter what you're going through? He never takes His eyes off you.

He loves you so much. He died for you because He yearns to form His image in you. Romans 8:29 says that God predestined us all "to be conformed to the image of His Son." Colossians 3:10 tells us that He wants us to be conformed to "a true knowledge" of His image.

He never takes His eyes off you. When you feel the worst you've ever felt, He's gazing at you. He wants you to have enough love and faith to look back at Him and see that He never stops looking at you and loving you.

And when that's your reality, you'll never want to take your eyes off Him because you'll have only one desire.

In Psalms 27:4, David essentially says, "I just have one thing I want to do. I want to gaze at Him. I want to fix my eyes on Him."

It's the same thing Jesus tells Martha in Luke 10. Mary, her sister, is sitting at Jesus' feet, leaning in, listening to Him, loving Him. Martha is so busy with the food preparations that she gets distracted and bothered. She forgets how much Jesus cares about her. She forgets that He is staring right into her eyes with great love and affection. She's so busy doing stuff, trying to impress Jesus. And she says, "Jesus, don't you care?"

Jesus says to Martha, "Martha, your sister Mary has chosen the one thing, the best thing." That "one thing" is sitting at the feet of Jesus, listening to Him, loving on Him, and letting Him love on you.

David has one thing he desires, and Mary chooses the one greatest priority, the one best thing. What's the "one thing"? Getting close enough to Jesus and staying there in His presence.

How close do I need to be?

Closer.

That's the one thing. Because if that's your life, how can you have a bad day?

You see how subtle this is? As you read this, I don't think you're tempted to go out and commit murder. I don't think you're contemplating whether or not you should go out and have an affair. You wouldn't be reading this if you did.

You know what most of us contemplate? So many Christians wonder if Jesus really loves them that much.

God's kids sometimes think, "I wonder if I'm really the apple of His eye. Am I really all that special to Him? I'm wondering if everything He said about me is really true."

That's our temptation because we always think we've got to measure up, and we can't.

We didn't all sign a petition that read, "God, would you please come down and save us?"

Coming to earth was His idea.

The Father knew that we were not going to get it, so He sent His Son, Jesus, to go for it anyway because He's love. He makes all the first moves. Aren't you glad He's love?

When we grasp this and live this—how much God loves us and cares about us, and the world—it changes the core of our being.

Mathew 5:8 tells us that pure-hearted people see God. Think about it. And Titus 1:15 says, "To the pure, all things are pure." When your heart is like His, you see the good in everybody and everything.

You don't say, "What's with that dirt bag? We gave him eight chances. Nine strikes, you're out." You don't do that. When your heart's pure, you look at them and see them as Jesus sees them no matter how far they're gone.

So David's out in the wilderness, killing lions and bears as a teenager, then he faces the giant Goliath. And he's not afraid because he knows the Lord is at his right hand. Why would the Lord stand by his right hand? Look Psalm 109:31. "He stands at the right hand of the needy, to save him from those who judge his soul."

What does that mean? Matthew 5:3 promises us that the poor in spirit are blessed by God because they get the kingdom of heaven.

If you let God know how desperate you are, He won't just look from heaven and gaze over the wall with the great cloud of witnesses. He'll come and stand right beside you and never let you go. He'll never leave you.

If you're desperate and poor in spirit, God won't leave you where you are. He'll come down and make Himself known to you. He'll stand right beside you and say, "I'm with him. Don't you dare mess with him. He belongs to Me."

Think about that. The Lord God Almighty is at my right hand. He is at your right hand. How can we be shaken when He is standing right beside us?

That word "shaken" is a word that describes emotions that arise from storms and trials and tribulations where you think that you're in over your head and you're not going to make it through. But when you realize that Jesus is with you, those things don't affect you anymore. In fact, the greater the onslaught coming against you, the more you sense His presence next to you.

It's the background of Psalms 84, where it states that though we walk through the "Valley of Baca" (which means the "Valley of Weeping"), if we keep walking by faith in Him, we will be greatly blessed. No matter what you're going through, it's not about what you're going through. It's about whom you're going with.

It's not about the fiery furnace that you're facing, or about it's being heated up seven times hotter. It's about who is in the fire with you.

When you realize that He's at your right hand, because you can't do it on your own, just stay poor in spirit—the humble attitude of a poor person. He'll never leave you or forsake you. He promised.

When you don't know who you are, you'll think it's about getting *your* breakthrough toward something better. When it's reduced to that, you're a person in need of the gospel.

So many churchgoers today think they need ongoing ministry. They want everybody else to pray for them. They want the prayer chain activated to get everybody praying for them. They're continually saying, "I'm going through a hard time. I need your help.

Would you pray for me? I'm really hurting." Where'd that come from? I thought Jesus was at your right hand. I thought you were the house of God and that Jesus lived inside you.

Flowing from God's Presence

What would happen if we just stayed in God's presence, and He said, "Go to this or that person," and you went and ministered to them as He directed, and then you came back and asked, "Now what?"

Then what if Jesus said to you, "Wait." And in patient obedience to Him, you wait.

Then after awhile He said, "Now go." You obeyed and you went and you came back. How could you ever get offended doing that? How could you ever get tired doing that? How can you wear out by flowing from God?

People say to me, "You're going to burn out."

"What do you mean burn out?"

"Well," they say, "You don't understand. We burn out. I mean, you've got to give your self some time and space."

Really? You don't think God can equip me to do what He sent me to do? Do you think God's limited?

Some people say, "Oh, you need to plan those times that you can get away and give yourself a break because even Jesus got away."

I appreciate the concern, but I'll take time off when God tells me to take time off, not when you tell me to get away, because you're operating from your perspective. And I'm trying to operate from His perspective. If I stay in His vision, listening to His Voice, then there's not a chance I'll ever burn out.

It's when I try to do things by my own willpower and not His power that I've always dried up and burned out. But when you drink out of my saucer, it's because my cup is overflowing, and I can't even begin to hold on to it. The Lord is constantly filling my cup, and I'm giving you the overflow.

I think we can get to a point where Satan is so afraid of getting his teeth kicked in when he comes around us that he will look at our street and say, "We're not going down this street because every time we do, that person rises up and says, 'Jesus is still with me.'"

Some say, "Are you sure we should be that bold about who we are in Jesus?"

Jesus would walk around, and the demonized people would say, "Don't mess with us yet, please. It's not yet our time to go into the abyss." Demons are petrified of Jesus. They shake in His presence, and He lives inside all of us who love and follow Him.

The problem is not what we're going through. The problem is who we believe we are.

David says because he knows that the Lord is at his right hand, he would never be shaken. Because David knows who he is in the Lord, and because he knows that the Lord will always be at his right hand, he says that his heart and his mind continually rejoice.

Our basic problem is who we believe we are, or that we forget who we really are. If you get to the point where you really trust Him in the big storm, then your mind starts rejoicing because you're already in His heart.

I rejoice because I've learned to speak over my reality, because the reality of my heart and my mind are now one, and because He's proved himself again and again.

I don't have to worry about it ever again. I'm finally getting to the place where I can obey His commands. Over and over Jesus commands us to not be afraid. Don't be afraid and don't worry about anything.

Don't Worry

Let's start with these two things that we should never worry about. Let's don't ever worry about Satan again, and let's don't ever worry about sin again. Let's start with those things because if we don't worry about them, then they have no jurisdiction over us. Then when a storm comes, we can say, "Good. Okay, God, I need some grace right here because I'm going to trust You. Because You said You'd never leave me or forsake me, and You'll get to that storm and turn it into my next windfall of blessing. I know, Lord, that you will work great good for me out of this storm."

Satan will have to try something different because now you're immune to that storm. It's kind of like a spiritual inoculation.

I don't need to go to a revival to get revived. I'm not arrogant. I'm not happy because my life's in order and everything's hunky dory. I'm happy because I realize who I really am in Christ.

Some would say in the natural realm, "I've had the hardest year I've ever had in my life." I understand that. But that part of you is temporary. The part of you that's forever can be experiencing the best year you have ever lived in the midst of the storms.

Every year you live can be the best year you have ever lived, eclipsing last year's great year. That's true all because of Jesus and His promises—if you really know who you are in Jesus.

I'm talking about your *becoming the message.*

Moreover, my flesh will also rest in hope. So not only my heart and my emotions and my mind, but now my flesh will rest in hope. Why? It's because Romans 5:3 says that trials will lead me to perseverance, and perseverance will lead me to Jesus-like character. Christlike character will lead me to hope. And hope will never disappoint me.

So bring it on, world. Bring it on, Satan. Because the more you bring it on, the more I'm in hope.

Some will say, "You're just looking for trouble."

No, I'm looking for Jesus. I'm forever realizing that He's gazing at me, and I never want to take my eyes off Him.

Peter's quoting David reminds us all that God will not leave our souls in hades (what many misconstrue as hell). Praise the Lord. This is why our souls never have to be shaken.

David says, "You will not abandon my soul to Hades." Why? Because Jesus says He's the way, and He's the truth and He's the life (John 14:6). He says He's in us just as He and the Father are in each other and are One (John 17:21). He says He will keep us safe from evil, from corruption (John 17:15). Deuteronomy 31:6 tells us, "Be strong and courageous, do not be afraid or tremble at them, for the LORD your God is the one who goes with you. He will not fail you or forsake you."

This great promise from God says that everything we do, we do together with Him because He will never leave us or forsake us.

So no matter if you go into the depths of hades, He hasn't left you. Even if you go through the Valley of the Shadow of Death, and sooner or later we all walk through that valley, He's still with us.

No matter how dark it is, no matter how stormy it is, no matter how impossible it looks, He's still with you. He will not let your soul be left in a pit. He will never leave you. He will never forsake you.

What you're going through is only a season that He's taking you through. He has a purpose. He will always lead you into triumph. He promised.

Victory in Trials

Why would God, our heavenly Father, who could prevent any sorrow or bad thing from happening, let bad things happen to us? Why does He let us go through tough times?

In our darkest times Jesus is our pattern. In our best and brightest times, Jesus is also our pattern.

In our darkest moments we should look at Jesus in His darkest moments to see how He gets through His worst times because He is our example, our model, and our pattern.

When Jesus is crucified, His Spirit goes into hades, and what He does while He's there is revealed in Colossians 2:15. That passage tells us that while He is in hades, He disarms the demonic principalities and renders them powerless. There's nothing they can do back to Him. Jesus could only do that by going and being where they were and conquering them there in hades.

I wonder if He allows us to go through hard things so that He can use us as His agents of stripping principalities and rendering them powerless in the places of those hard situations.

I wonder if He allows you to go through things that you would never wish on your worst enemy because He loves you so much, and He wants to give you the incredible experience of rendering demons powerless in His name and by His power.

He wants you to be a part of His redemption of all things. He wants to take you through enough battles and trials until you finally realize it's not about you and what you're going through, but it's all about Him and the victory He gives us in all things. He uses those trials to make us strong in the power of His might.

When you realize who's going through the trials with you and how He's growing you in them, you'll no longer look at circumstances and say, "When will this trial ever end?" Instead, you start looking at Jesus.

You start asking Him, "What are we going to do next? What victories will we enjoy together? Into what new triumph are You leading me through this trial? What unexpected blessings are you preparing for me through this trial?"

If you come down with a sickness, you can say, "I trust You to heal this, Jesus." If somebody gets hurt, your response can be, "This will lead to a miracle, won't it, Jesus?"

Let's imagine that you lose your job. You can trust Jesus and say, "You have a new job lined up for me, don't you, Jesus?"

Someone might say, "What do you mean by that, Dan? Are you one of those prosperity guys? I'm a Bible guy."

It has everything to do with the Bible. If you're in God's hands, and He's taking you with Him, and He'll never leave you or forsake you, then the worst situation you can imagine could become the best experience in the world because it's with Him. He promised to work great good for you out of the worst that ever happens to you.

This is what I believe happens in Acts 16:24 where Paul and Silas are locked in the "inner prison." Satan thinks he's silenced these two mighty men of God. They're beaten badly with rods and stuck in the "inner prison," which by the nature of a Roman prison is probably the cesspool for the whole prison. It's a dark, dank, wet, disease-infected dungeon.

God allows this to happen to His faithful witnesses—on purpose. His purpose. Satan thinks that he's finally got Paul and Silas beat. He has no idea that God's power will be released through their mighty praise and worship. Our Lord intends to use Paul and Silas to save the jailer and his entire household.

The Greek word here for "inner" is *esoteran*. It is used in only two places in the New Testament, here referring to a prison, and in Hebrews, where it describes the entrance to the Holy of Holies. Think about that.

Your darkest "dungeon" can be your entrance into "The Most Holy Place" in the entire cosmos. This is only possible because Jesus is always with you, no matter what.

You are not on planet earth for your ease and comfort. The reason God breathes into your nostrils and gives you life is so He can manifest His love through you to a dying world.

When you fully realize who you truly are in Christ, and you realize why He still has you breathing on earth, then you'll stop measuring His love and favor by what you're going through. You'll start measuring His favor by how much He trusts you to go through for Him, especially for the cause of saving others.

Your worst situation can be the closest place to the Holy of Holies.

Spirit-Anointed Life

Peter isn't even a good preacher. He's a fisherman, and when the crowd hears his Pentecost sermon, they say, "Oh my word, what do we have to do?"

When you preach the whole gospel—the Word and the Spirit, the holiness and the healing, the doctrine and the display—people get convicted by God, and they want to repent. When you preach the whole message, people can't resist it. Three thousand of them get saved that day. They repent, they get baptized, they get filled with the Holy Spirit.

The world was never the same. This was the birthday of the church of Jesus Christ.

Three thousand get saved on the Day of Pentecost after Peter's sermon, and the believers practice their new faith by breaking of bread (eating meals together), fellowshipping, praying, and listening to the apostle's teachings.

What does that tell us? It reminds us that it's not enough to get baptized in the Spirit and operate in the power of the gifts of the Spirit. The believers continue by doing the same things that got them into the position of blessing and anointing in the first place.

"A sense of awe" comes upon every soul (2:43), and many signs and wonders are done through the apostles. The same things that Jesus did while He ministered on earth are now going on through the apostles—through the same Spirit. They have genuine *agape* love for one another. They have unity of faith. And they will turn the world upside down in their lifetimes.

In Acts 3 Peter and John are continually being filled by the Holy Spirit every day. They're living a revival.

When you go to work tomorrow, and you don't have the church crowd around you, and you're sitting there all alone, Jesus is with you. You don't have to wait for revival to come because there's already revival in you. His name is Jesus. He's inside you.

I understand we want to see cities fall at the feet of Jesus in passionate worship of Him. But until that happens, what about the person in front of you? Revival is wherever you are because Jesus is in you. Revival is in you. It has nothing to do with what you're going through. It has everything to do with whom you're with.

You don't have to concern yourself with whether anybody accepts you or not. With Jesus in you, you can love them to death.

We used to say that we need to preach the hell out of people. No, let's just love the hell out of them. You can't preach anything out of anybody. But they can't resist Jesus' *agape* love in you.

Peter and John are walking by the gate to the temple in Jerusalem. They're going to a prayer meeting because they don't want to stop praying.

A man who was lame from his mother's womb is carried every day to that gate and left there to beg all day long. When Peter and

John see him, he asks for money. Peter fixes his eyes on this pathetic man and tells him to focus on them. So the beggar gives them his attention, expecting to receive something.

Peter tells him he doesn't have any silver and gold for him. Peter is not relying on what he can do. He's not relying on his circumstances. He's not relying on money or resources. He's not relying on how many Bible verses he read that morning. He's not relying on his perfect church attendance. He's not relying on whether he pleased the pastor. He's not relying on what he doesn't have.

Dear Christian, you're not owned by this world. This world has nothing to do with who you really are. You're possessed by the King of kings. God is here right now. He's right where you are reading this book. He is with you. He wants to do something in you that changes your eternity right now.

First Peter 2:24 says we die to sin and live to righteousness. The fruit of righteousness is holiness. The fruit of holiness is eternal life. You're in it forever.

Some might say, "What if I sin?"

I don't know. Maybe you have a god who won't forgive you. But if Jesus is your God, and if you confess that sin, you know He is faithful and just to forgive you. And He will cleanse you from all sin and unrighteousness (1 John 1:7–9).

Do you see how stupid we get? I don't want to sin. I don't even want to think about it. That's the last thing I want to think about. I'm not going to think about what I could do. I'm going to focus on who He says I am.

So Peter says to the lame man, "I do not possess silver and gold, but what I do have I give to you: In the name of Jesus Christ the Nazarene, walk."

The Greek word for "walk" is the word *peripateo*. It means to "walk around," and it's also used to describe or teach us how to live or conduct ourselves. We don't lag behind Him in life. We don't get ahead of Him when we preach. We live the life of the New Covenant and by the Spirit, instead of by the flesh.

You have the remedy for people's physical conditions—the healing that Jesus offers. And you have the remedy for people's spiritual conditions—you're the gate of heaven because of who you are in Jesus.

You might as well start believing it.

My Prayer–Your Prayer

Here is an extended prayer from my heart. May it also be yours.

"Lord, would You teach me what it means to fall so in love with You that I become Your temple, Your precious, intimate dwelling place? I want to become a channel that You flow through. Jesus, I want to lay out my life the way You did. Would you show me what it looks like? It has to be attainable, or You wouldn't have led me to this place in life. It has to be sustainable, or You wouldn't have commanded it.

"God, we know that you won't dangle carrots in front of us that are unattainable because love doesn't do that.

"There has to be a way, God, that we can walk in continued intimacy with unbroken awareness of Your presence in our lives. It can't be something that's turned on and off, depending on which room we're in. Let us walk in 24/7 unbroken fellowship with you, Abba Father, so that wherever we are, we reflect You and represent You as Jesus did.

"Lord Jesus, we may be somewhere in public, like at a store, and we hear the Spirit say, 'Pray for that person.' And we instantly obey the Spirit's prompting. Help us to be so obedient to Your voice, dear God.

"Abba, we don't have to have a healing service because we *are* the healing service, and we walk it out in our neighborhood. God, we don't have to ask people, 'Would you come to church?' Because we are the church. This has to be the reality of our lives, God.

"This has to be the reality of our lives, dear Jesus. We cannot do this on our own. We cannot accomplish this or live like this out of sheer discipline, will power, and effort. Lord God, You must do it in us. You must make us daily fall in love with Jesus on a deeper level—deeper than we have ever loved You, Jesus.

"Wake us up!

"Wake us up to who we really are in You, Jesus.

"Help us to live up to what You bought for us with Your precious, priceless, powerful blood.

"Let us live up to what You expected when You saved us.

"Remind us constantly throughout the day that we are Your dwelling place. Help us to never forget that You live right inside us.

"Lord Jesus, help us not to live with multiple choices and multiple options. Let us live with a singleness of focus in mind. It's all for You, Jesus. It's all for Your glory. We may not see everything that we want to see, but love never fails.

"Mighty Savior, we don't need to be emotional. We just need to be real and believe this. May we trust and obey You regardless of circumstances.

"Help us to remember that everybody responds to Your presence differently and individually. Some may cry, others may have goose bumps, or somebody may shout. Other followers of You may not feel anything.

"Lord, in Your grace and mercy, help us fall so madly in love with You that Your presence is unmistakable, whether we feel anything or not. Jesus, we want to be one with You. We want our identity to be *in You*. Amen."

Let's give love away. Let's give Jesus.

About the Author

Dan Bohi is the founder of Becoming Love Ministries Assoc-iation (formerly Dan Bohi Ministries Association) and his mission is awaken the church of Jesus Christ to the power, purity, and freedom of the Spirit-Filled life, found, realized, experienced and exhibited in the lives of believers in the Book of Acts! He is the co-author of Holiness and Healing. Dan has traveled the country for 12 years imparting the message of Holiness to pastors, leaders and churches in 22 different denominations.

If you would like to contact Dan
for a speaking event please visit :
www.BecomingLoveMinistries.com
or contact Rev. Jim Williams at:
JimWilliams@BecomingLoveMinistries.com

Becoming Love Ministries
7905 NW 48th St.
Bethany, OK 73008